God Doesn't Have a Trophy Case

Refocusing Christianity

Brian Nogay

God Doesn't Have A Trophy Case
by Brian Nogay

Printed in the United States of America

ISBN 1-59781-979-4

Unless otherwise indicated, Bible quotations are taken from:

Saint Joseph Edition of The New American Bible, Catholic Book Publishing Company, New York Copyright © 1992

Self-Pronouncing Edition, The Holy Bible King James Version, Christian Heritage Publishing Company, Inc,. © 1988

www.xulonpress.com

Table of Contents

Page

7	Chapter 1	Being Recognized
19	Chapter 2	Explaining the Unknown
31	Chapter 3	The Ten Commandments
43	Chapter 4	The Structure of Belief
53	Chapter 5	Using God as Justification
65	Chapter 6	Historical Jesus
75	Chapter 7	What is God's Message?
87	Chapter 8	The Road to God is Straight and Narrow
99	Chapter 9	Making their God our God
113	Chapter 10	Personal Relationships

125   Chapter 11   Putting God in our life

139   Chapter 12   Contact with God

151   Chapter 13   Faith and Action

165   Chapter 14   What we control: Actions and
                      Reactions

177   Chapter 15   Grace

191   Chapter 16   Our lives are a preparation
                      for the kingdom

203   Chapter 17   Finding God: Not exactly
                      what we expect

215   Chapter 18   God is the Interruption

227   Chapter 19   God's will. What should
                      we do?

239   Chapter 20   Playing God

251   Chapter 21   Civility

263   Chapter 22   Discerning versus judgmental

277   Chapter 23   Building Community

293   Chapter 24   Meek does not mean timid

307   Chapter 25   What Matters

CHAPTER ONE

Being Recognized

During the graduation ceremony for over 200 senior high students of Our Lady of Good Counsel High School at Constitution Hall in Washington, D.C., the school administration gave out awards for excellence in English, Math, Science, and all the other disciplines. From my seat in the faculty section, I watched as awards were also given for leadership, service, Christian character and several other character traits. The number of awards given out totaled twenty-three, not including the athletic awards presented at another ceremony.

While the ceremony continued, my mind started wandering and I began to think about all the awards given out in business, entertainment, television, movies, radio, theater, the print medium, and athletics. Winning an Oscar, Emmy, Grammy, Golden Globe, or championship, and being named the Most Valuable Player in any sport or activity meant being the best, being number one. Making it to the top of the rankings and getting elected into the appropriate "Hall of Fame" seemed to be the ultimate goal and the highest possible reward. As I sat there lost in thought, I wondered how much God cared about those awards and I couldn't help but ask myself what God recognizes us for.

Recognizing deserving individuals for their excellence seemed appropriate, but the presentations also seemed to create the expectation of being rewarded for achievements and accomplishments. It was as though doing anything really important, such as having the highest grade point average in the class or getting involved in the most activities would get the student recognized, and maybe even a trophy.

Those students hoped to be chosen for awards at their graduation, and we all aspire to be honored as the most valuable player on our team, employee of the month, and citizen, coach, or volunteer of the year. We measure accomplishment by getting a promotion, an increase in salary, a bigger house, a nicer car or a more prestigious job title. We measure our success based on what we achieve and often equate achievement with what we own or what we can put in our trophy case. In general we tend to validate ourselves through our trophies and our social status. We often assume the most important behaviors will bring us attention and reward.

We have special cups, animal heads or skins, medals, bowling or swimming trophies, pins, buttons, badges, ribbons, newspaper clippings, photographs, autographs, pressed flowers, and memorabilia. As we get older we might also accumulate less obvious trophies, such as expensive cars, yachts, antiques, attractive spouses, splendid homes and vacation cottages, college degrees, impressive high-status jobs, and so on. They all essentially serve the same purpose as our third-grade spelling-bee medal: to bolster our feelings of self-worth and self-importance. This is the "I am what I own" school of self-esteem, the idea that achievement is measured by the acquisition of material possessions.

The slogan of this school of thought is, "He who dies with the most toys, wins" but what do we win? Actor Matt Damon, as quoted in an interview by Dotson Rader in Parade Magazine in November 2003, remembered being alone and staring at his Oscar for the movie *Good Will Hunting*. He stated, "People go their whole lives chasing after this thing, thinking it will give them happiness, when it isn't true. It doesn't. For me, the next few years were a process of learning what does."[1] For all of us our lives are a process of learning what does bring us happiness and fulfillment. If we attain power, popularity, influence, wealth, luxury, and fame and still aren't more satisfied, fulfilled, secure, and happy with our lives it is because these items fail to measure our worth, as God might.

God's sense of accomplishment is very different from ours. God doesn't feel the need to "prove" God's worth, and perhaps we shouldn't feel that way either, especially if we are trying to get closer to God. If we are serious about creating a deeper relationship with God, we'll notice that God doesn't bother with outward displays of worth. God doesn't have a trophy case. God doesn't collect; God gives. We tend to accumulate; God disseminates. We horde; God generously distributes love and forgiveness. We reflect our self-worth; God gives us limitless opportunities to enhance our worth.

Since antiquity, people have searched for ways to feel good and attempt to attain happiness through comfort and pleasure. King Ludwig built the castle called Newschwanstein in the mountains of Germany which served as the inspiration for the Walt Disney castle at Disneyworld and is believed to have committed suicide. Worldly possessions could not bring him to love his life. St. Augustine "collected" physical pleasures as a young man in pursuit of a sense of self, only to give up all worldly goods and hedonistic experiences for a devoutly spiritual life; that's why we remember him.

It's the same way with people we admire such as Mother Theresa and Albert Schweitzer. They gave of themselves until it hurt and kept on giving. Somehow, these people went from collecting material items and being concerned with awards and material comfort to being concerned with accomplishment from God's perspective.

Accomplishments

At seven thirty mass one morning at St. Bernadette Church, Fr. Thompson delivered a homily regarding the following story. A minister was looking through the obituaries one day and noticed a strange similarity between two death notices. The first was for a Mr. Blessed. The obituary read: Mr. Blessed was accomplished in golf and won numerous Club Championships. Upon retirement he dedicated himself to improving his golf game and won several Senior Club championships. He is survived by his wife and three children.

The second obituary was for a Mr. Holy. The obituary read: Mr. Holy was active in his community and volunteered at regional soup kitchens and shelters. Upon retirement he dedicated himself to the welfare of society and the betterment of humanity through community service. He is survived by his wife and two children.

The minister noticed the similarity between the two obituaries and concluded that they must have been written by the same individual who simply filled in the specific information about each person on certain lines. If that template awaits all of us for our obituaries, what could be filled in on those lines describing our lives in a few words and what would we want them to say?

As we consider our own mortality it is up to us to provide the material to summarize our lives. While in no way discounting our ability to spend our leisure time as we see fit and the legitimate value of golf or any other activity, what do we consider to be the most important information when describing our lives? What do we spend our time involved in and dedicate ourselves to? The question we must ask ourselves is do we evaluate our lives by the contents of our trophy case, or by what we have accomplished in God's terms?

Our trophy case is full of what we have done in the past. The medal we won in high school track, the silver cup for second place in the debate contest ten years ago, and all the other items we have collected to some extent define us but what do they have to do with God?

God doesn't have an enormous trophy inscribed with "Number One" or "Champion" on it, even though God could possess the biggest and best trophy ever to reflect its relative importance. Engraved on God's trophy could be the words: "Created and Saved humanity." Jesus didn't receive even one participation ribbon or plaque, let alone a championship trophy, yet surely he was deserving of a huge reward, something better than a crown of thorns.

When we summarize our lives we should consider whether we are working toward a full trophy case or toward heaven. If we want a full trophy case, we should direct all our energy toward that end and compete in lots of contests and competitions, both official and unofficial. If we want to be Christians we should direct our energy toward reward, achievement, and recognition from perspective of the Supreme Being we call God.

From god to God

God can show us where the real trophies are. Our primary concern should be acknowledgement of the fact that God exists; understanding God is a lifelong journey. God is medicine, not anesthetic. God is not a tourniquet which cuts off our connection to life but the medical stint by which we become more open to the life possible. God does not anaesthetize us and deaden us from our frailties, shortcomings, and imperfections; God heightens our awareness to the possibilities of true accomplishment in our life.

Birds flying in the air, fish swimming in the waters, and beasts wandering the land were all mysterious to early humans struggling to comprehend the world around them.

Because there was little scientific knowledge to explain the world factually and mankind needed answers, belief systems and faiths developed throughout the recorded history of mankind to explain the world and life.

Supreme beings became responsible for forces of nature and nature itself. Man created gods as ultimate powers over existence. Humans made up reasons for why things happened without knowing if those explanations were right or wrong. The desire to know and explain the world led Ancient Egyptians and Greeks to create mythologies to provide answers for that which they did not understand.

When we try to explain the world and our existence, we are trying to find answers. God might represent our personal answer to the unknown and our attempt to explain just who is in charge of this life, just as early Greek culture invented gods such as Zeus and his wife Hera to represent the ultimate beings in control over the other gods and the universe. The mood and nature of these distant gods was punitive and unforgiving, leading people to live in constant fear.

Superstition led humans to believe that their behavior was constantly evaluated by the gods and destructive events resulted if the gods weren't constantly appeased. A superstition is an irrational belief in the cause and effect of why events take place, such as the contention that the rainfall which brought about a plentiful harvest meant that the gods were pleased, and natural disasters such as destructive volcanoes, floods, hurricanes and droughts indicated the god's displeasure. Superstitions occur even today without our knowledge such as the belief that God watches over us making a check-list of our mistakes in order to punish us.

Natural events were thought to be based on the moods and whims of the gods. Speculation abounded, leading to the creation of many myths. A myth is a made-up explanation of natural phenomena such as the belief that the sun rose in the morning through the power of the sun god. Claude Levi-Strauss in *The Raw and the Cooked,* states, "I therefore claim to show, not how men think in myths, but how myths operate in men's minds without their being aware of the fact."

An ancient's belief that a volcano erupted because a god was angry is similar to a modern man's belief that his lucky shorts are responsible for his making the winning shot at a basketball game. It's also similar to our belief that our relationship with God and our salvation are obtainable only through certain rituals, special prayers, or the rites within a certain religion by following directions to "earn" God's blessings, such as attending mass every Sunday or contributing money to the church.

Science has gradually provided factual explanations for many formerly supernatural occurrences and reduced these events to natural facts but we still seek to understand, find meaning, and explain the unknown through God. Today we might find the idea of a sun god or rain god to be humorous, but if we "believe" in God without feeling any personal sense of connection to God; if our concept of God is the result of someone else's belief rather than our own; we may be allowing myths to operate in our mind without even being aware of the fact, and we might as well pray to Thor or Hera.

Jocelyn Bell-Brunell, a Professor of Astrophysics at Open University in England, said, "I think the human brain stores problems, things it can't resolve, things it can't cope with." Maybe explaining the unknown and finding the meaning of life are questions we cannot cope with and which are stored in our brain until we resolve them. The Big Questions for early man and for us are still the same: What is the meaning of life and why are we here? God can provide us with answers to those questions.

A believer in God concerns herself with something more than this physical space. Her sense of religion connects her to God, and in turn she feels connected to the world around her seeing beyond what is visible. As John Muir once said, if you pick a wildflower, you will find the entire universe attached to its roots. Jewish symbolism commonly represents being rooted in God by showing an upside-down tree. The person who believes in God understands this connection to something in addition to this physical place and sees God as a way to find answers.

If God represents the creator of all life, then God represents what is most important and how we find true achievement and accomplishment. If God has all the answers and finding true meaning is possible through God, then making our picture of God clearer is critical to help us find what true accomplishment is.

Reasons for Having God

As children grow up, they need to know why events happen. They want to know why they have to go to the doctor and get a shot if they aren't sick or why the family has to go to Aunt Mary's house for Thanksgiving. Children reach a stage when they are three or four years old when they constantly ask, "Why?" "Why is the sky blue?" "Why do we have two legs and dogs have four legs; why does an apple fall from a tree but the moon stay up in the sky?" This is an attempt to find answers for what they cannot comprehend.

In the same way we attempt to find answers to what we don't understand. We need a guide to what is important because our self-worth is based on our accomplishments. God can provide us with answers as we struggle to find a reason for living, a purpose for our existence, and an explanation for why we are here.

Knowing God exists and is with us can also give us the same feeling of comfort a child gets from a loving parent. A parent will find through personal experience that their small children will play by themselves, even if they are in a room away from their parents, as long as they believe that their parents are close by. However, if they do not think their parents are nearby, the children may feel abandoned and begin to cry.

Children seek out their parents to provide them with safety and comfort when they are afraid. Similarly, we depend on God to provide us with security and reassurance when we are afraid. God makes us feel cared for and protected. The idea that the ultimate force in the universe is a personal, caring being gives us great comfort.

Animals and plants have mechanisms to help insure survival of the species. Female animals from dogs to Japanese Beetles emit sex-attractant chemicals called pheromones to attract males to mate. Plants such as dandelions have seeds shaped so that any wind or animal contact will scatter the seeds long distances. Flowers have petals of vibrant colors to attract bees to help them pollinate and produce new offspring.

Having children, seeing them grow and have children of their own helps us see the continual process of life. Children can reassure us that others will carry on our genetic legacy, our ideas, and continue our existence after we are dead. We want our personal life to continue. Our soul, our spirit, that other part of us is the means by which we will live on after our physical bodies die. Could belief in God be a survival mechanism man developed to avoid the depressing possibility that this life is all there is? In an effort to make us immortal, God allows us to continue our existence on another plane. God offers us eternal life in Heaven. The reward of an afterlife is a trophy and the hope of that reward brings us joy and comfort.

The possibility that our existence begins and ends with our earthly life may lead us to feel detached, alone, isolated, depressed, and without hope. If our discovery of God is simply a way to escape despair and experience its opposite, joy, the experience of joy through belief in God is still joy. If God provides the trophy we seek but we do not understand how, does it matter?

Walter Lewin, a physicist at the Massachusetts Institute of Technology stated, "Physics describes things, describes phenomena, and as long as it is predictable, as long as the formalism applied in a certain situation gives you the right answer, who cares, who cares what the meaning is of understanding? Who cares? I leave that up to philosophers. I think they don't have a clue, either."

If God provides us with the answer to the question of accomplishment in our life, if God is our explanation of the unknown; does it matter if we know why? The modern miracle of refrigeration makes air conditioning and food storage possible for all people, although few understand how refrigeration works. Nevertheless, refrigeration exists and is available for the benefit of everyone. In the same way, God also exists and is available to everyone, whether we understand "how" or "why" or not.

CHAPTER TWO

Explaining the Unknown

Richard Henry Stoddard wrote: "We have two lives about us, two worlds in which we dwell, within us and without us, alternate Heaven and Hell: Without, the somber real, within our heart of hearts, the beautiful ideal." Our life, our entire existence, is a journey spent attempting to find ultimate meaning (God) and reach perfection (Heaven) while avoiding distraction (the Devil) and ending up lost (in Hell). The clearer we are about what God represents, the better idea we will have about the meaning of life. We have various ways of finding happiness, joy, and peace and many maps at our disposal because religions, churches, and theological scholars offer us many explanations of God. God represents the beautiful ideal of our life and our existence.

God

God is the ultimate power, our representation of life's creator. Any symbol that makes our picture of God sharper serves its purpose to help us understand the character and nature of God. The Star of David to Judaism, the Cross to Christianity; the ancient Jews didn't even speak God's name because of their complete reverence and high regard for the creator and Orthodox Jews still do not even speak God's name. Today on the internet some Jewish websites refer to God by writing G-d.

In *World Waiting to be Born,* Dr. Scott Peck writes: *"The person with a secular mentality feels himself to be the center of the universe. Yet he is likely to suffer from a sense of meaninglessness and insignificance, being one out of six billion people on this planet. The person with a sacred mentality, on the other hand, does not feel herself to be the center of the universe. She considers the center to be elsewhere and other. Western religions designate the other to be God."*[2]

In the attempt to define who the ultimate being was, Eastern beliefs (Hinduism, Buddhism, and Confucianism) developed a focus on the personal inner being, truth, and consciousness as means of dealing with life and forces not under our control. This philosophical quest for meaning, insight, and knowledge centered on personal discovery as more of a philosophy of reality than an explanation of supernatural forces, beings, or spirituality. The gods of the Hindu and Buddhist faiths were often portrayed as distant, detached, unemotional, unconcerned, and sometimes amoral rulers characterized like a painter who, after creating mankind, was "finished" with humanity and not continually involved.

Western religions (Judaism, Islam, and Christianity) developed belief in one superior being called God (monotheism). In these religions, God was much more clearly defined than previously. The Hebrew culture humanized God and spoke of a caring, active deity like a caring father who was not only involved in our lives but who loved us and was available to help us.

This ethical monotheism was different from other religions in that it placed emphasis on the way other people were treated. The Hebrews also believed God would send a savior, a Messiah, to save the Jews. Today, Jews await the arrival of this savior from God. Christians believe Jesus Christ is the promised Messiah. Muslims consider Jesus a prophet but see Muhammad as God's chosen messenger, to whom God dictated the holy book of Islam, the Koran.

Eastern and Western religions were led to different explanations of the unknown and a different view of the ultimate trophy giver, the almighty, as if people were looking at the same object through the same prism but seeing the object in a different way, or perhaps seeing only a certain portion or segment of the object. The object offering an explanation of the unknown is the same for all monotheistic religions: the object is God.

We must answer the question of who we think God is for ourselves, and this is difficult since God is all things. God is not a portion; God is the whole.

If we are at a salad bar and pick and choose what we like, we have not made *the* salad, we have made *our* salad; we have made a portion of what exists. Although we construct our own idea of who God is, we do not make God; God is, whether we admit it or not, and God does not cease to exist if we don't believe in God.

G.C. Lichtenberg said, "God created man in his own image says the Bible; philosophers reverse the process: they create God in theirs." Rather than preoccupying ourselves about rules, routines, and rituals we need to perform to get to God, our goal should be to arrive at our own relationship with the ultimate power in the universe and thereby find personal meaning in our own lives.

Our God is constructed within our capabilities. Our house, whether wood, brick, sand, or stone, is built within the limitations of that material. A driver in a Humvee can go different places than the driver in a Volkswagen, but each must be aware of the limits of what they have. Our definition and image of God is formed according to our experiences and our own secular, Muslim, Jewish, or Christian perspective.

Many people imagine God as an elderly white man in the clouds of heaven, who seems like a distant ominous judge. However, what God represents is much more important than how we think God might look. God is more important than God's form. Whether we imagine a spirit, being, or powerful force, the Christian God represents hope, love, perfect joy, and peace. The Christian God is made very clear through the teachings of Jesus Christ, and the place where God resides and where we end up if we are faithful to God is referred to as Heaven.

Heaven

Heaven is where we will experience God. What is it like? People who have had a near-death experience describe heaven in terms of great light, warmth, peace, and an overwhelming feeling of contentment or lack of want. Classical Christian images of heaven often depict a kingdom in the clouds where angels float around unhurried, almost in slow motion, displaying a curious partiality to white, flowing robes and who seem to be experiencing great peace and contentment.

Members of most faiths believe in some sort of continuation of life. Reincarnation is an ancient belief which originated in India in the 9th Century B.C. as one explanation of how life would continue. Reincarnation beliefs differ but all have to do with existence in an altered state whether as another human being or as a dog, rat, cow, tree or spirit. Reincarnation represents an alternative to Heaven.

Jehovah's Witnesses believe that a finite number of people will be saved and taken to heaven (140,000) while the rest will enjoy the blessings of life here on earth. The Buddha used to describe life's goal as he saw it in the word Nirvana. *"Nirvana is the highest destiny of the human spirit and its literal meaning is extinction, but we must be precise about what will be extinguished. It is the boundaries of the finite self. It does not follow that what will be left is nothing.*

Negatively, nirvana is the state in which the faggots of private desire have been completely consumed and everything that restricts the boundless life has died. Affirmatively, it is that boundless life itself."[3]

Heaven is an ideal of this "boundless life" which helps people focus on where we end up after this life, a sort of ultimate trophy to be attained by our life here on earth. But we don't know if Heaven is actually a place, a condition, or a state of being. Just as our creator God represents our ideal of ultimate perfection, peace, contentment, and bliss; Heaven represents where God and these feelings can be experienced. The result of not attaining this goal would be a place without God.

Hell

The word "Hell" was not used in the original texts of either the Old Testament, which was written in Hebrew, or the New Testament which was written in Greek. There is a curious alteration of words in the translation from both these original languages into English. "Hell" was the word chosen by translators to convey what they thought was the appropriate meaning of "being without God."

The ancient Jewish people were prohibited from reading the Word of God, which could only be read by the clergy. The learned attempted to illustrate God, Heaven, Hell, and the Devil for the uneducated. Symbols of Heaven and Hell were also used to motivate Pagans to join Judaism or Christianity, and such examples helped the church hierarchy convey their meaning through references that the people could relate to. Hence, the city of Jerusalem represented the saved world, what the people knew as the center of life, and Hell was where people would be without God.

The word *hell* in old English means to conceal, hide, or cover, and in literature there are references to such actions as the "helling" of potatoes. The word Hell shows up thirty one times in the Old Testament after translation into English. It conjures up images of darkness, suffocation, isolation, and death as the most horrible physical place the people of that time could relate to. Hell illustrates the horrors of the state of detachment from God.

Ancient Egyptians had a central location where the dead were taken for disposal. This place was separated from the other parts of the city of Cairo by water and was similar in function to a city dump or landfill of today. Biblical references to "Gehenna" refer to a "grave" or "pit," which was the repository for things with no value. Gehenna was just such a city dump in the Valley of Hinnom in Jerusalem during the times of the Bible writings. Executed criminals and socially deposed people were disposed of in a dump or pit such as Gehenna.

Some of the Sanhedrin (the 71 learned judges of Judaism) sometimes denied burial to particularly grievous offenders and their bodies were thrown together with the carcasses of dogs, city refuse, and other waste into Gehenna where a fire burned the trash. Any material that did not make it into the pit was eaten by worms around the sides of the pit.

The moral of the story was that opposition to God would result in the loss of hope and a gruesome and horrible fate.

The lesson was for people to be redeemed and brought to the full knowledge of truth by choosing God and religion over any other belief system. Hell was a state of guilt, hopelessness, meaninglessness, torment, pain and anguish, lack of control, silence, and oblivion resulting from being separated from God. For people of that age, a vision of Hell as the place outside of a city where garbage (useless material stripped of all worth) was burned and destroyed could not have made Hell any clearer. Even the uneducated of the time could relate to that description of the consequences of detaching oneself from God.

As time went by, various Christian sects became more and more specific about the characteristics of Hell, such as was described in Dante's famous *Inferno*. Ancient Jews were extremely concerned with purification rites, necessary before entering the Temple. The idea of Purgatory is a Catholic belief similar in nature to the ritual cleansing of the Jews, even though Purgatory is after death.

Purgatory is a state of "cleansing" for all of us sinners, plus people such as unbaptized babies and "good pagans" such as in the Bible story of the good Samaritan who stopped and attended to the needs of a severely beaten and bleeding Jew even though many Jews passed by the man. Purgatory is a cleansing, altering, or changing similar in meaning to the Nirvana of the Buddha where we change from our sinful desires and attitudes to God's attitudes.

Purgatory represents a decontamination holding cell to eventually make us clean enough to possess the perspective to think like God.

Heaven saves us from the hell of emptiness and isolation from God. Gerald Vann writes in *The Pain and the Sorrow of Christ*: "Hell is essentially a state of being which we fashion for ourselves: a final state of separateness from God which is the result not of God's repudiation of man, but of man's repudiation of God."[4]

Scott Peck wrote in *People of the Lie*: "*Evil is perpetrated by people who are absolutely certain of what they are doing. Evil people are 'the people of the lie,' deceiving others as they also build layer upon layer of self-deception. While evil people are still to be feared, they are also to be pitied. Forever fleeing the light of self-exposure and the voice of their own conscience, they are the most frightened of human beings. They need not be consigned to any hell; they are already in it.*"[5]

In our search for meaning and God we are empowered by being given the choice to follow God or not. As C.S. Lewis remarked in *The Great Divorce*, God does not punish us; we punish ourselves and essentially put ourselves in hell. We essentially choose to be with God in Heaven or without God in Hell.

The Devil

According to scripture, God made Archangels to perform special functions and the devil was originally one of those Angels. Lucifer was intended to help mankind and was made to test mankind's gift of free will but instead desired equality with God and was banished from Heaven. He became the victim of his own free will when he chose to oppose God. Lucifer was the name given to what we call Venus, the morning star in Roman astronomy. Equating Lucifer with Satan is a mistranslation but the being now referred to as Satan represents opposition to God, as a fallen angel who knew God but chose to go against God.

If the Devil, also called Beelzebub or Lucifer, is the opposite of God, then all of the Devil's characteristics can be assumed to be the opposite of the terms which describe God. The Devil therefore represents selfishness, deceit, fear, hatred, pain, mystery, emptiness and meaninglessness.

The Devil represents Hell because he is aware of the love of God but does not feel it. Our life's journey involves continually seeking God, but distractions can keep us from that reality and lead us down the self-centered path that Lucifer took. Lucifer craved total power and understanding, but we do not have to have all the answers. God is our representation of all understanding and the all-powerful, and we do not have to know "why." To develop spiritually, we must only admit we need God's assistance, we must only admit that God is the higher power. The Devil represents the constant temptation which keeps us from concentrating on God.

If we seek closeness to God, Heaven is where we will be with God, Hell is where we will be without God and the Devil will tempt us and keep us from attaining these ideals. Our lives are the preparation as well as the trip to reach contentment and our journey to Heaven becomes our destination. Organized religions speak of Heaven and God as if they are trophies obtainable to us after this life if we follow their rules, but are God, Heaven, Hell, and the Devil people, places, and things; or are they possibilities we can bring into our world through how we act?

Staying away from Hell and the Devil requires us to concentrate on getting closer to God and doing God's will, but what does God want? What are the rules for following God?

CHAPTER THREE

The Ten Commandments

The Ten Commandments, which many of us are familiar with, are the "decrees" in the Judeo-Christian religious tradition, handed down to the Hebrews thousands of years ago. As the basic building block of religious teachings, these rules are assumed by many to be the most important things we could do, the big fundamentals, the ultimate guide to following God's wishes and having a positive relationship with the almighty. But if we take a good look at these commandments and if we are honest, we will conclude that we actually pick, choose, rationalize, and justify what amounts to breaking many if not most of them. If the Commandments represent the foundation of our religious beliefs, then a lot of us are in a whole lot of trouble. Exodus 20:2-17 lists the Ten Commandments as:

I am the Lord your God, you shall not have false
    gods before me.
Do not make idols of any kind to worship.
Do not use God's name in vain.
Keep Holy the Sabbath.
Honor your mother and father.
Do not kill.
Do not commit adultery.
Do not steal.
Do not lie.
Do not covet your neighbor's wife or your neigh-
    bor's possessions.

At first glance, these commandments seem like
a list of behaviors to be avoided, a do-not-do list
instead of a list of guidelines to follow. They may
make us uneasy because they are a list of restrictions
set before us like a huge boulder, but they require
no personal involvement, especially emotional
involvement on our part. If we recall that the Ten
Commandments were given to Moses and presented
to an outcast people who were very unclear about who
or what God was, and who were in much physical
and emotional pain, the undeniable fact is that the list
shows that God found the Jewish people pleasing.
The Commandments provided the Jewish people
with an outline of how to follow God, a means of
being worthy of God's love and they can provide us
with the same outline of how to get closer to God.

**I am the Lord your God and you shall not have
false gods before me.** The result of hearing these
words today might make us intolerant of others and

might lead us to believe that God is telling us, "I'm the real one and all those others are wrong." Some interpretations even use the words *strange gods*, as in "You shall not have strange gods before me," making it sound as though God is telling us to "Pick me and stay away from all the weird ones."

Is this command about God controlling us, or was the command simply an attempt to explain God's singular form to people struggling with the very concept of God thousands of years ago? This commandment actually represents a drastic departure from the beliefs in many gods (polytheism) and their shared domination of the universe to belief in the consolidated power of one God.

These words were given to people who had previously believed in the powers of a myriad of gods and supernatural beings that controlled the world. The belief systems of those times were lacking the scientific knowledge and consciousness we have today. Therefore, we should not interpret the commandment as a restriction or evidence of God's intolerance but a reminder for us to prioritize the one true God as the most important concern of our lives, the one trophy worth seeking.

We must admit that we do not control everything and admit that the ultimate authority is God. Our boss-employee relationship and a parent-child relationship require knowing who is in charge, but that is administrative detail. Our relationship with God is a vertical one, with God above us. A church sign board said: "To understand God we must stand under God." God is perfect and the rest of us are human. All our other relationships, whether with individuals or institutions, should be horizontal ones where we give and take along the same human level.

Do not make idols of any kind to worship. The commandment says not to make idols or images of anything, not to worship anything in the same way as God and not to hold anything as important as God thousands of years ago when some of the Jews began to worship the Golden Calf. The word idol is sometimes replaced by the words "graven images." Graven (which means engraved or carved) conjures up unknown but menacing forces to be avoided. These words most certainly were used to incite fear in the ancient Hebrews. The inference to keep God number one or else was probably meant to scare people into believing in God.

As we in capitalist societies buy our newest toy, we may not be abiding by this commandment. Our car, our house, our status (which we allow to become something we cannot live without), any *thing* we like a little too much, may be the idol we worship. When we look at our car, home, or our high-definition, wide-screen television with DVD player, we must ask ourselves if we love it so much that it is the biggest priority in our lives.

There is no material object that deserves the same adoration that we give God. In other words, we should not allow anything we own to own us. This commandment sounds like a warning to maintain a healthy perspective on what matters most to us and to not become obsessed with what we own. God should be the only thing we can't live without.

Do not use the name of God in vain. Oh God; that's a tough one! No using the name of God in vain? If this is one of the really big sins, most of us are in big trouble. What percent of us are guilty of saying "God" when we aren't trying to get the Lord's attention? A teacher once told me that when we use the name of God, God responds by saying, "Yes, what do you want?"

When we say the word but do not want God's attention, it's like someone calling our name but not trying to contact us at all. Therefore it shows disrespect and trivializes the role God has in our lives. The story of the little boy who cried "Wolf" to see if the shepherd would really come to his rescue cried, "Wolf" so many times that the shepherd thought the boy was pretending when the wolf actually did show up. Imagine if God reacted to us like the shepherd and failed to respond when we really wanted God's help.

How literally should we take this commandment? Do we need to count how many times we've violated it? Perhaps this commandment refers more to our impudent, disrespectful attitude toward the Creator rather than to specific examples of saying the word "God" without reverence. If God represents our creator, why are we degrading that image, and if we believe we are made by God why are we degrading ourselves?

Remember to keep Holy the Sabbath. This instruction tells us to keep the Sabbath holy. This commandment is a request for us to keep a proper perspective on where we are in our life. It was also an effort to prevent overwork and abuse of slaves and animals in Jesus' time. After creating the heavens and the earth, God rested. Keeping the Sabbath holy involves stopping whatever activities we are doing to rest and reflect. The "Sabbath" means a day of worship and religion for Jews and refers to Friday evening until Saturday before sunset.

If we don't keep Saturday holy, we are apparently breaking a commandment. Islam uses Friday as the day of worship and Christian denominations worship on Sunday. Christians celebrate on Sunday because, after Jesus' death, Christians wanted to separate themselves from the Jews, therefore they chose a different day to worship the Lord.

The Sabbath allows us to give time and honor to God. If we walk nonstop with our head down, we not only lose sight of where we are going but we can't even see where we are. As we travel through our lives, periodically stopping to rest allows us the opportunity to keep focused on what ultimate achievement is. Do we rest and dedicate a day to the Lord, or are we guilty of violating this guideline also?

Honor your mother and father. This commandment tells us to honor and respect our parents and to hold the people who bore us in high regard, which sounds like a reasonable request, but if we have abusive parents, what then? What honor are we to give them if they emotionally, physically, or sexually abuse us? Honoring our father and mother leads us to respect and appreciate both males and females as parents and partners in the gift of our life. This declaration exhorts us to treat our parents with respect, just as we respect our Heavenly Father as our creator.

Honoring the male and female as basic parts of the human family unit is a way for us to respect humanity and be thankful for our life.

Thou shall not kill. This is possibly the most straight-forward and easy to understand of all the commandments, but wait, have we ever stepped on a bug? That disease-laden fly in our kitchen, the chicken or steer that just provided us with the meat we ate for dinner, the leather shoes or clothes we wear, do they count? Even John the Baptist ate locusts with wild honey. We need to reflect on how literally we interpret this command. If we actually think about all forms of killing, are any of us innocent of this one? This commandment, given to people thousands of years ago, made it very clear to respect all life.

Some versions of the Bible state "thou shall not murder" rather than "thou shall not kill." If we maintain a reverence and appreciation for life, we can separate what actions we take for our survival (which includes eating living plants for our salad and pasta) from purposeful or malicious killing.

Do not commit adultery. An astounding percentage of people are supposed to have committed adultery but every source differs. According to "Affair Statistics" by Karen S. Peterson of USA Today about 24% of men and 14% of women have had sex outside of marriage.[6] "About Lovers & Other Strangers"[7] shows much higher statistics-as many as 50% to 65% of men having affairs, and William (Bill) Mitchell documented 50% to 70% of infidelity in the last decade in "Adultery, Facing Its Reality."[8]

It is impossible to measure the reliability of any data related to sexual relationships between married people, but it should be clear from these studies that infidelity is common. The ancient meaning of adultery as sexual intercourse between those who were not married to each other also included sex outside of marriage, or fornication.

We are taught about sex at an early age. This commandment doesn't say sex is bad; it says that breaking a sacred vow with another person (and possibly exposing him or her to disease) is bad. It was probably difficult for the writers of the Torah to imagine a woman committing adultery, since the lives of women were so controlled by their parents and husbands.

Former President Carter was quoted as being repentant for committing adultery in his mind, that is, thinking about a woman sexually. Adultery is a violation of commitment, a cheapening of God in the body. Adultery involves betrayal, disloyalty, and dishonesty. With regard to our honor, the commandment is an illustration of how good our word or vow is.

Thou shall not steal. This commandment is pretty all-inclusive; however do we simply ignore this commandment when it's convenient for us? We can justify the act of taking that which doesn't belong to us and rationalize our actions. Getting around the law and doing something to benefit ourselves regardless of the degree ranges from stealing millions as a corporate officer to saving a few dollars by being dishonest with our taxes.

Is one instance worse than the other? What about the moral dilemma of stealing food to survive, is that included too, and if so, is it wrong? The commandment is clear that taking what is not rightfully ours is wrong. We are expected to work for and earn what we obtain.

Thou shall not bear false witness. The focus of this commandment is to be truthful and honest with ourselves and others. It is very specific: Don't lie about a person or event that we know the truth about. It does not mention circumstances or conditions; it simply tells us to have personal integrity and be truthful in whatever we do. There is no exception stated here, even though there are plenty implied. We might interpret this commandment to read: do not lie.

We might tell a child that her dog ran away instead of telling her it was hit by a car and rationalize being dishonest by claiming it was done for her own good (to spare her pain), or even say our lie was a harmless "little white lie." The problem is that we justify lying even when we don't honestly have the other person's feelings foremost in our minds; but this commandment includes lying to ourselves. The black Americans who claimed hundreds of thousands of dollars on their tax returns and called it remuneration for slavery, mislead themselves to justify taking money which was not theirs.

We mislead each other constantly and often mislead ourselves. We all have our reasons for lying, even though, just as with stealing, the commandment directs us in no uncertain terms not to misrepresent ourselves. We spend a lot of time and energy rationalizing our actions and only we know how much we lie and deceive. Maybe, instead of lying we should call our duplicitous actions a lack of honesty or integrity. False witness has to do with misrepresenting information, or ourselves, including the act of taking advantage of another person.

Thou shall not covet your neighbor's wife, or things. The commandment reminds us to be accountable for our actions, take what we earn, and not be concerned with what other people possess. The fact that two out of the Ten Commandments are concerned with sexual activity shows the importance and priority that sex has. Coveting is jealousy. We are not supposed to covet (desire or yearn for) another man's wife or possessions. The focus of this directive is to simply not want what someone else has. If we desire another person's possessions, we aren't satisfied with what we have ourselves. This commandment is God's demand for us to take personal responsibility for everything in our lives.

If we can move away from fear and avoidance of these Commandments, we might stop feeling so persecuted and focus on how we can become closer to God. Consider the circumstances of the creation of the Commandments: given by God to a great, humble man, very basic in nature and unmediated, they were rules for wilderness survival for a large group.

Maybe the presentation of these messages contained in the Commandments has obscured their message. The original intent of the words, which came directly from God, might be different from what we receive. Maybe God isn't standing watch over us, checking off the rules we violate, but trying to assist us to get to Heaven. Christians or Jews may fear God's wrath if the commandments are broken, but most are easy to keep. Christianity and Judaism also allow for repentance and forgiveness of our sins, allowing every person to start over and try again.

The Ten Commandments are behaviors to follow, not actions to avoid. The Commandments can become a reference guide for our benefit if we see them as a way to stay focused on character issues and virtues that will keep us heading toward God. The list concerns us personally, because these rules are not imposed on us by others or God but because we should impose them on ourselves. The Commandments require us to be personally involved in our actions because they tell us not through superstition or routine, but through cause and effect that certain behaviors will separate us from God. The Commandments make clear how we develop a relationship with God.

CHAPTER FOUR

The structure of Belief

Because of man's desire to attain a high state of consciousness, heighten his awareness and put God into a more accessible form, people developed a tendency to create or build something to represent God. Ancient peoples felt that monuments were needed to show respect to their gods. Sacrificial altars were a common part of early civilizations, including the Mayan and ancient Hebrew cultures. The Pyramids were monuments to the Pharaohs, who were considered to be gods themselves. In Europe, a town had to have a Cathedral to be considered a city. Large Cathedrals and Churches were built to honor God, but also to impress the masses.

The expectation of reward includes the perception that if we do what religions tell us and follow their directions, God and heaven are our reward. The massive Cathedral of Notre Dame in Paris was built to honor God but also to remind the downtrodden that, if they were faithful to the Church, a reward like the Cathedral awaited them. Their reward was Heaven and monuments themselves became trophies.

Memorials and monuments are reminders of what we hold in especially high regard and these memorials can enrich our relationship with God. However, if our attention is on the monument rather than on God, it can distract us from our belief and become an idol itself. Our journey to God is like a maze that we create. We create distance between ourselves and God by creating paths we must follow to contact God.

For example, to communicate with God, we devise mythical steps we must follow, and we superstitiously assume that if those procedures are not followed, we can't reach God. Religions formulate rituals, rules, and regulations to be followed so that our communication with God can be completed. We may then believe that God only becomes available through those procedures.

Organized religion is the form we follow for worship and religion like a school where we can learn more about God; an owner's manual on how to do what God wants. Sacraments, Commandments, tenets, precepts, and the Five Pillars of Islam are seen as fundamental user's guides to believers. Holy books such as the Torah, the Koran, the Book of Mormon, and the Bible, are especially revered as God's word by the believers of those respective religions.

The Bible is a translated collaborative effort put together by a group of individuals hundreds of years after Jesus' death. Fundamentalist Baptists believe in the Bible literally while Episcopalians, Lutherans,

Presbyterians and Catholics allow for some interpretation of the text. Because the Bible is a "group" effort, Muslims consider the Bible to be "contaminated' by man's interpretation and input and they point to the Koran as an unadulterated direct dictation by God to Muhammad.

The Koran outlines acceptable and forbidden behaviors as a code of daily living for Muslims. The Torah, the basis for the Jewish faith, is God's word through the prophets. The Torah accounts for the first five books of the Old Testament of the Christian Bible. The Torah, or Law is the first section of the Old Testament. The Prophets, and the Writings make up the rest of the scripture. The Christian Bible consists of the Old Testament, the Gospels written about the life and teachings of Jesus of Nazareth, plus books about the lives of the Apostles written after Jesus' death and resurrection.

As we pursue a relationship with God and attempt to get to Heaven, we need assistance and guidelines. If God is our ultimate destination, the form we seek, and if we have made the decision to find life's meaning through God, then every monument, rule, ritual, and regulation should remind us of God and every moment become an opportunity to reflect our relationship with God. Rituals differ from faith to faith, but rituals should serve the same purpose: to bring us closer to God. We run into trouble when the items and rituals we use to bring us closer to God achieve "trophy" status themselves.

When ritual becomes practiced for its own sake, it becomes worship of an object, or idolatry. We may be reminded of God as we dip our hand in holy water, sit, kneel, stand, genuflect, recite words and bow down, or we may be focused on the form we follow, the ritual performance of our routines. This leads to a market for all sorts of beads, trinkets, procedures, and related "holy items," because contact with God is then based on the routine we follow or the item we use in the routine such as the rosary beads or the medallion we wear rather than the earnestness of our heart.

The faith we practice then becomes the routine we must follow to achieve our trophy.

We must have the perspective to worship God through the reminder such as the beautiful church or valuable rosary beads and not put value on the church or rosary beads themselves. Our Temples, Mosques, Churches, Synagogues, Shrines, and Cathedrals are places where we worship, but they are not what we worship.

We must be aware that whatever we create might lead us farther away from God instead of closer. A one hundred page instruction manual called the General Instruction for the Roman Missel brought out by the Catholic church in January of 2004 describes specifics of the mass such as how all altar cloth's must be white, servers may wear only white vestments (robes), and large crosses are not allowed to be worn by the servers.

Religions dictate what is acceptable to believers both in terms of thoughts and actions. Religions delineate what is acceptable through rules, regulations, and views on the entire range of human activities, from athletics to ethics. For instance, birth control and abortion are both forbidden by the Catholic Church and chastity, or abstinence from sex is the only permitted option to sex.

Other religions have their own restrictions. For example, alcohol and tobacco are prohibited by Islam. There are restrictions on the use of medicine by Scientologists. Generations ago, singing and dancing was prohibited by fundamental Baptists. The consumption of Coke and Caffeine was forbidden in the Mormon Church until the church purchased a portion of the company in the late 20th century.

Many faiths fast during Lent. Jewish purification rituals were central to being allowed to enter and worship in the Temple, the structure central to the Jewish faith and culture which was destroyed two thousand years ago even though the rituals do not apply to synagogues. A Kippah, a small cap called a Yarmulke, was worn by the high priest and when Judaism came to regard every person as a high priest and each table as an altar, the wearing of a Yarmulke became a public way for each individual to remember and acknowledge their association with God.

Jehovah's witnesses believe that the Catholic belief in the Trinity (the Father, son Jesus, and the Holy Spirit being three parts of the same entity), is a false belief started by the devil himself and shows the sinfulness of Catholicism. Polygamy was also a part of the Muslim and Mormon faiths in the past.

Statues of St. Francis or St. Jude are to remind Catholics of how those individuals lived so we can remember their examples. The purpose of holy items is to help us focus on our relationship with God. It is like having a poster of our favorite all-star athlete hanging on the wall of our room to give us something to aspire to.

Each religion is a pathway to God. Each believes in a very specific nature of God and each claim's to be the correct method to get to God. Put into a more defined structure, our methods become our religion and we can develop the belief that our church is the only one, our prayer the only correct one, and our ability to reach God depends on using our trinkets or beads. We can then believe the myth that if we want God to give us a trophy or reward, we have to follow the criteria established by that religion.

Belief systems can develop a possessive attitude about God and act as if people have to do things a certain way to contact God. At this point a sense of obligation begins to interfere with our contact with God. Our interaction is then determined through and possibly obscured by religious scholars, theologians, members of religious hierarchy, religious institutions, ceremonial customs and organizational procedures. This misconception leads us to become more concerned with how we do things (the form or appearance) than what we do (the function of contacting God and doing God's will).

In time, we may begin to believe that unless we attend Temple, Church, or Mosque, or Synagogue we can't get through to God. This can lead us to believe that we have to be in Church or Temple to make contact with God, or that simply by being in the Temple, Church, Mosque, or Synagogue building we are fulfilling our obligation to God. We can also believe that our obligation to the church is the same as our obligation to God. None of these conclusions are true, however; they are the result of placing too much importance on the procedure we use to contact God.

A father was driving his mini-van to one of the endless errands of a busy day. His young daughter said, "Daddy, we're coming up to the cloud."

"The what?" the man said.

"The cloud," the girl repeated.

"What are you talking about? What cloud?"

"The section of road up here is so smooth, it's like a cloud." As he went over that portion of road the man noticed it was much smoother than the other sections of road.

Over the next few months the man found himself anticipating the section of road his daughter pointed out and thinking about his daughter every time he went over it. Eventually he looked forward to that section of road and found himself smiling at the thought of his daughter as he drove over it. Even after a harsh winter formed a pot-hole in "the cloud," making it not-so-perfect, he still thought of his daughter every time he went over that section of road. The road itself was not important to the man but the man used the road as a catalyst for thinking about his daughter.

Imperfections exist in reminders of God, but as long as we think about God, every "prop" serves its purpose. Each faith and belief system provides what those individuals believe is the correct method for reaching God, but procedures and routines are only meaningful if they have significance to us personally.

When John, a parochial school student, brings home religion books to study for a test, he spends hours memorizing and reciting all sorts of prayers and rote statements such as: "Our job for God is to know Him, to love Him, and to serve Him." The main purpose of this type of instruction seems to be aimed at indoctrinating John in the procedures of the church and its belief's but what seems to be missing is the message. John donates $5.00 to the Tsunami Relief efforts and raises money in the Walk-For-The -Homeless but purposely fails to invite several class-mates to the movies because he's mad at them.

As part of his religion homework assignments, John is told rules, regulations, rituals of his faith and what is holy, what is sacred, and what his obligations are for his particular religion, but he is not always told why those things are holy, sacred, or required.

As John memorizes the correct responses for lessons of the faith, that faith should be personalized. Religion homework should apply to our life. John could be asked how God would hope he acts when he sees a new kid sitting alone at lunch, or if he treated anyone badly on the playground at recess that day. How he answers would force him to see how every action he performs reflects his faith and personalizes his relationship with God to the people he is with and the people in front of him.

Two elderly Catholic women were talking about an acquaintance named Pat when one stated, "You know, she's Catholic, but she's not a practicing Catholic." What she meant was that Pat didn't attend mass, but what was implied was that since Pat didn't attend mass, she wasn't practicing her faith.

Are we to assume then that a practicing Catholic attends mass, or is any practicing Christian one who acts out Jesus' message of service? Human nature makes us want to enhance our belief, change it, and make it into a restrictive social group, but our personal relationship with God is ours alone. Our obligation is to God, not to the church. When procedure becomes more important than worshipping God, our faith can even become a weapon to be used against others.

Because Jesus himself broke Jewish law by healing on the Sabbath, the high priests saw this as the highest violation of their religious code and set out to arrest him. Jesus angered many of the church leaders but his perspective was clear. The persecution of Jesus was initiated because he did not follow the established procedures, Jewish traditions and Roman law. He interpreted the law himself and determined that it was more important for him to assist those he saw in need than to obey the letter of Jewish law regarding rest on the Sabbath and Roman law regarding insurrection.

We also need to consider how we reflect our belief in God every day. How do we react when someone wants to switch lanes in front of us on the way home from work? How do we react when the person in front of us is taking too long in the checkout line at the grocery store? How do we react when watching our kids play a soccer game and see the referee make what we think is a terrible call?

Every faith believes themselves to be the correct, chosen, or favored ones like the ancient Jews believed. Jesus taught that all are chosen, but only a few respond. In Acts 10:34-35 the Bible says, "Every nation who fears him and acts uprightly is acceptable." Corinthians 3:3-4 states: "Have no divisions. Each of you is saying, 'I belong to Paul' or 'I belong to Apollos.' Is Christ divided? Was Paul crucified for you?

Galatians 3:27-28 states: "There is neither Jew nor Greek, there is neither slave nor free, for you are all one in Jesus Christ." We all belong to God and God is the salvation of all people. As Christians, we should look past the differences in form of our denominational faith and be concerned with the commonality of our belief in God.

If God is a gift to mankind, then religions are the packages and the wrapping. The packages might be different on the outside but all have the worship of God inside. The true test of following God's will is the practice of faith, not the colored paper, bows and procedural adornments that faith is wrapped up in. But God's will is not as clear as we might believe, because throughout history mankind has defended his actions by claiming to be performing God's will. So what is God's will?

CHAPTER FIVE

Using God as justification

❧

Throughout history, from Moses to King David to Constantine to Hitler, God has been used as the justification of both good and evil to justify the imposition of one man's will upon another. As Ancient civilizations struggled to survive and were sometimes subjugated by force and repression, belief systems and religions shaped human history.

Even today, throughout the world, people have freedoms restricted by individuals and groups claiming to speak for God and who claim to be acting on God's behalf. Adolph Hitler claimed to be inter- vening on God's behalf by initiating the Holocaust, the attempted extermination of the Jewish people. In his Reichstag Speech of 1936 he said, "Today, I believe that I am acting in accordance with the will of the almighty Creator: by defending myself against the Jew, I am fighting for the work of the Lord."

Thousands of years ago, as the Jewish people were forced to wander for 40 years in the Sinai Desert, their belief in God provided them with hope. Their belief in God sustained them and gave them strength during oppression and extended periods of hardship. Belief that they were God's chosen people provided them with a reason to stay together and persevere. Even after the Romans destroyed the Temple, which was the central symbol for social, religious, cultural, and economic organization and identity for the Jews, their belief in God unified them.

In ancient times, the region of the Middle East referred to as the Arab world was a chaotic coexistence of related peoples with many belief systems. Lawlessness and polytheism were rampant. In the seventh century A.D. the prophet Muhammad founded Islam, a strict, monotheistic religion, and within a century the belief in one God (Allah) spread throughout Arabia. Islam extended its influence over an area greater than that of the Roman Empire at its height.

After executing the Jew, Jesus himself, and persecuting the followers of Jesus Christ for four hundred years, the Roman Empire adopted the Catholic Church as the official state religion when the Roman emperor Constantine converted to Christianity. Even today the religion is known as the Roman Catholic Church.

The Roman Empire attempted to protect its rule and expand its power throughout its history. The Catholic Church initiated the Crusades in 1096 to return the Holy Lands to Christianity and to forcefully convert Muslims to Christianity. To gain acceptance for the Crusades, the Pope and church leaders claimed to be enacting God's will.

The Inquisition was a church body established by the Papacy in the twelfth century and made an official church body in 1231 to oppose dissenters and punish "heretics," or anyone who believed in any opinion that contradicted established religious teachings.

Since the state determined which religion was acceptable, any person refusing to follow the state mandated religion (Roman Catholicism), was seen as an enemy of the state and was sought out and punished. The Spanish Inquisition, a judicial institution established by the Papacy in 1478 at the request of King Ferdinand, was state sponsored religious persecution which sought out heretics in Spain until 1834.

The brutality and injustice of this church body served to force religion on people and attempted to dictate what individuals believed even if scientific facts contradicted the belief. Galileo espoused the Copernican thinking that the sun and not the earth was the center of the solar system. Papal authorities responded to his findings by coercing him to kneel and recant his beliefs. The church placed him under house arrest because his findings contradicted Church teachings, essentially censuring him to force his "obedience."

The code of behavior in the Koran is used in varying degrees, depending upon whether it is practiced by a radical or fundamental sect. One part is called *Sharia,* in which Islamic Law states that the punishment for stealing is the loss of a hand and the punishment for *zina,* adultery or illegal sex, is being stoned to death while being buried up to the waist.

In the 13th century, the behavior of the Pope and Papal families (including wives and children of Pope's), the wealth of the church, tax-free possessions, greed, and immorality of the hierarchy (which owned from one-fifth to one-third the lands of Europe at that time) incited the peasantry to revolt.

During the Reformation, Protestant denominations were established in reaction to the power and sovereignty of the Roman Catholic Church. Christian denominations other than the Catholic Church continued following the teachings of Jesus Christ while separating themselves from the Papal governance of the Catholic Church.

These protestant churches conducted persecutions of their own in the Protestant Inquisitions as each church began to define their beliefs more clearly and defend them more vigorously. They became increasingly intolerant of differing views and became, and remain today, a splintered group of related but separate sects. In the 14th century John Wycliffe, an English reformer, spoke out against the papacy for the sale of indulgences (forgiveness of sins) and the corruption of the church hierarchy. He translated the Bible into English to make it more accessible to the commoners.

In the early 16th century Martin Luther, the founder of the Lutheran Church, defied the authority of the Catholic Church. He protested the colonial nature of the church because it collected money from the church in Germany, England, France, and Spain. He reacted against the taxing and forced obedience to Rome and the Pope as head of the church. John Knox started the Presbyterian Church and took the new religion to Britain.

The United States of America was founded as a country that would not endorse or mandate a state religion but would allow an individual to worship in their own way, without state interference. The United States was a realization of the words of Frederick the Great who said, "All religions must be tolerated, for every man must get to heaven in his own way."

The separation of church and state was established to protect an individual's right to practice the religion of his or her choice. Church and state were set apart from one another, not to isolate or eliminate organized religion, as was the case in the Soviet Union, but to guarantee tolerance for and inclusion of all religious beliefs. God was guaranteed a place in, not removed from society.

In 2003 in Georgia, a stone display of the Ten Commandments was removed from the state courthouse to supposedly enforce this separation of church and state, with the court claiming that the display was a state endorsement of religion, but the development seemingly contradicts the intent of the founding fathers.

The Ancient Greek Philosopher Plutarch said, "God is the brave man's hope and not the coward's excuse" but desperate individuals still invoke religion and God to justify evil or terrorist actions. John Krakauer's 2003 book *Under the Banner of Heaven,* which focuses on one man who murdered a woman and her young daughter, delves into the religious fanaticism of fundamentalists who, though excommunicated from the Mormon Church, still believed in the practice of polygamy and thought that they could speak directly to God.

Even today the man who carried out these crimes has no remorse because he claims to have carried out God's will in committing the murders. Such a stance is reminiscent of Osama Bin Laden, who claimed to be enacting the will of Allah when he masterminded numerous attacks against the United States on September 11, 2001 when airliners were flown into the World Trade Centers, the Pentagon, and into the Pennsylvania countryside.

Sacred Trust

Numerous parish priests have been found to be pedophiles who abused numerous children. Cardinal Bernard Law of Boston and Edward Egan of New York knowingly covered up information and reassigned priests allowing them to continue abusing and putting other children at risk. Evangelists Jim and Tammy Baker stole millions of dollars from their church ministry, and President Clinton and Jesse Jackson had extramarital affairs and covered this information up. Hearing about this never ending scandal can shake our faith. It should not shake our faith in God, but our faith in people.

When people to whom we give a sacred trust violate that trust, we can lose hope in God. As we live through the horror of September 11, 2001, hear about massacres and genocide in other parts of the world, see other terrorist attacks and hear about deranged killers murdering innocent people, we can begin to doubt the goodness of God. We can even blame God and wonder how God can allow this evil to happen. We can even begin to believe God isn't so great, or that God doesn't exist because the people and religions who claim to represent God are so flawed and imperfect.

In 2000 a twenty-one-year old Palestinian woman from the West Bank drove her car up to a military check-point and blew herself up. She had told her family, "If I'm going to die at the hands of the Israelis anyway, why shouldn't I take some of them with me?" In a picture in the Washington Post, the girl was shown holding a dagger in one hand and holding up one finger signifying Allah with the other. Her uncle stated that even though he tried to reason with her he could not find strong arguments against hers.

The righteous and moral such as King David, Abraham, and Saint Peter are on the path to God, but except for the exemplary lives of a few saints, even individuals revered as pillars of faith and the church have committed some serious sins. God's messengers and those pretending to be god's messengers have always been imperfect.

Abraham, the common link between Islam, Judaism, and Christianity, is called the father of faith by three of the largest religions in the world, but Abraham lied that his wife was his sister and allowed her to be "given" to another King because Abraham feared the King would have him killed if he found out she was his wife. But Abraham was sorry for what he did and was forgiven by God. Abraham was even willing to sacrifice his own son to show his faith (although God spared the boy).

King David coveted Bethsheba, another man's wife, and sent her husband to the battlefield to be killed. David later admitted his transgressions and was repentant, he deferred to God, and this made him special in God's eyes. Because be was King, David didn't have to admit any wrongdoing. He even built monuments, not to himself, but in homage to God.

St. Peter denied Christ three times to protect himself and spare his own life when Jesus was about to be crucified, but later became "The Rock," the first Pope chosen by Jesus to lead the church. These men were all favored because, even though they sinned and failed as we do, their attitude was one of contrition and deference to God and God forgave them their sins. They placed God first in their lives. They were, as we are, imperfect and forgiven.

With even the most revered individuals of major religions so fallible, the imperfection of God's team is easy to see and point out. It seems that God's team of followers was never composed of All-Stars. Those average people who had faith and willingness to serve God were the people Jesus associated with: commoners, outcasts, prostitutes and those of low social standing, like fishermen and tax collectors. To the casual observer, it must have looked as if Jesus was forced to pick his team last.

What color are our glasses?

To many people, belief in God and religion is unrealistic because the world is so filled with evil and injustice. As we try to make sense of this world and why people act so inhumanely, it is difficult to be positive. Dr. Scott Peck, a psychiatrist and author of many books, writes in *The Road Less Traveled*: "As much as we may try to see the world through rose colored glasses, it probably makes more sense to assume this is a naturally evil world that has somehow been mysteriously 'contaminated' by goodness, rather than the other way around. The mystery of good is even greater than the mystery of evil."[9]

Dr. Peck doesn't use the word *bad,* he uses *evil.* Goodness is the opposite of evil. Goodness is that which promotes life and liveliness and evil is opposition to life. Dr. Peck created a nonprofit organization, The Foundation for Community Encouragement which attempts (according to its web-site) to build "Authentic relationships between individuals in community." He approaches life as a Christian, seeing the need for all of us to admit to a higher power. He writes that we must admit we do not control the world, and our understanding of reality is not something we achieve; it is only something that can be approached. Mental health requires that the human will submit itself to something higher than itself.

"...Mental health is an ongoing process of dedication to reality at all costs. Healing is the result of love and a function of love.

Health is not so much the absence of disease as it is the presence of the optimal healing process. We need to experience pain for our health and healing.

Salvation literally means "healing." Jesus taught us to pay less heed to ourselves in many ways (clothing, food, security), and more attention to the quality of prayer and our own faults. Evil people refuse to acknowledge their own failures, and actually desire to project their evil onto others and it is no wonder that children will misinterpret the process by hating themselves.

To receive treatment, one must want it, and acknowledge his or her own imperfection. The evil in this world is committed by the spiritual fat-cats, by the Pharisees of our own day, the self-righteous who think they are without sin because they are unwilling to suffer the discomfort of significant self-examination.

The denial of suffering is, in fact, a better definition of illness than its acceptance. The evil attack others instead of facing their own failures, they scapegoat. Spiritual growth requires the acknowledgement of one's own need to grow. We become evil by attempting to hide from ourselves. Laziness or the desire to escape "legitimate suffering" lies at the root of all mental illness. The essential psychological problem of human evil...is a variety of narcissism, or self-absorption, selfishness, and conceit." [10]

We all have a personal relationship with God, but if our faith does not give us joy and satisfaction, it is ineffective. If our relationship with God leads us to feel hopeless, give up and give in to death and murder, it is meaningless. Does our God condone murder and suicide? Do we believe God is glad to be associated with any of these violent, hateful, and hurtful situations? While we must define God in our own terms, what does our God make us feel?

Our idea of God and the characteristics of that God will be the rationale for our actions. Each individual must arrive at his or her own personal nature of God, but we will reap what we sow. We can act out of hate and anger, imposing fear to bring death through the power of destructive force, or we can act through the power of love as Mother Theresa did when she lovingly held a dying woman lying in the street of Calcutta so that for a moment the woman would know she was loved. The Christian God does not inflict pain; the Christian God represents love. The characteristics of the Christian God were brought into focus by the Jewish carpenter born in Bethlehem.

CHAPTER SIX

Historical Jesus

Throughout history, numerous prophets and religious leaders have attempted to tell us about the nature of God, what God is like, and what God wants as well as the rules of following God. The Torah and the Bible are records of the ancient Jews and early Christians as told by writers and men of means, who compiled, interpreted and documented events as the Word of God. John Smith in the Book of Mormon and Muhammad in the Koran also tell us about God.

Jesus of Nazareth was different. He claimed to be the son of God. Whereas other religions and views of God are based on "second-hand information," Christianity bases itself on the life and teachings of Jesus the Christ, who claimed to be God's son sent to earth to save mankind and provide first-hand information about God. Jesus asked his disciples, "Who do you say that I am?" and we have to answer the same question to fully understand the mystery of God's presence in our lives.

Jesus was a Jewish peasant carpenter born in the Mediterranean region about 4 B.C.. The world Jesus was born into was a cold and brutal one. Life was incredibly harsh for all but very few people and life expectancy was grim at best. Probably 33% of children born alive were dead before they reached the age of six. By sixteen, 60% would have died; 75% by 26, 90% by 46, and 97% before their 60's.[11]

Society was dictated by the influential and powerful who made all the rules. Might meant right. There was no moral or ethical direction outside of belief systems such as Judaism and Hinduism, only force. Peasants were subjected to severe social and economic stratification. They were left out of society, had only meager means to survive, and most of what they had was taxed or taken from them by the ruling Romans. The world they knew was cold and impersonal.

There was no such thing as personal rights, social justice, or the possibility of being able to move up the social ladder. Their society did not offer individuals protected freedoms or social mobility. The harsh life of peasants, tradesmen and laborers was not much more than a physical existence. There seemed to be no hope for the people at the bottom of the social ladder. Resources and influence were guarded forcefully by the few who had them.

At the time of Jesus, the Jews had been under the rule of the Romans for several generations. Jews themselves were divided as to how they dealt with their oppression. Some were outlaws who wanted rebellion; they were freedom fighters who attempted to wreak havoc on the Romans and overthrow society. The Sadducees, the Jews who were relatively high up on the societal ladder, attempted to adopt the ruling culture and make the best of the situation. Pharisees attempted to keep Judaism alive within the society by strict adherence to its codes and laws.

Another group, the Essenes, essentially withdrew from society and formed their own communes. Cynics espoused the abandonment of society, and Stoics detached themselves from the world in an attempt to escape the pain of existence altogether. Jesus was a peasant Jewish Cynic. Jewish Cynics were the Hippies of their day, fighting political and religious power to create a different kind of society.

By today's standards life was brutally difficult for Jesus and his contemporary peasants. Their options seemed to be limited to death, slavery, or banditry. In his book *The Historical Jesus,* John Dominic Crossan states, "People were suppressed to such a degree that they thought little of submitting to death, if only they could avoid calling any man master."[12] It was common in the Roman world of the Mediterranean during that time for infants to be left in rubbish heaps or to be saved to be reared as slaves. Peasants were thrown to lions, burned alive, even crucified to set a public example of consequences of opposing Roman rule.

Historically, several thousand people who claimed to be the Messiah were savagely beaten and crucified by the Romans to send a message to the Jews that opposition to Roman rule would result in torture and pain. Jesus was only one insurrectionist among many that the Roman's executed, but one thing set Jesus apart: his message of love. Jesus explained what the ultimate trophy was: to be with God in Heaven where we would attain peace and contentment.

Jesus brought a message explaining our personal salvation and taught about having access to God and heaven regardless of our circumstances in life and being with God for eternity. What made Jesus so different was his desire not for charity but a new society of equality and commensality, the creation of a kingdom of perfect mutual concern for each other.

It was not only what he said and taught but how he lived his message that clarified people's idea of God by narrowing the characteristics of God to an involved, loving, passionate, merciful, forgiving parent. He preached for three years and was arrested as an insurrectionist, crucified on Good Friday and rose from the dead on Easter Sunday. Jesus' message was for his disciples to love each other and to help others not only when the disciples felt like helping but whenever others needed help. Jesus provided assistance to the needy. Matthew 11:2 - 6, 18 tells us that:

> *"When John the Baptist heard in prison about the things that Christ was doing, he sent some of his disciples to him. 'Tell us, they asked Jesus, 'Are you the one John said was going to come, or should we expect someone else?' Jesus answered, 'Go back and tell John what you are hearing and what you are*

seeing: the blind can see, the lame can walk, those who suffer from dreaded skin diseases are made clean, the deaf hear, the dead are brought back to life, and the Good News is preached to the poor.'"

The *Mishnah* is a book of the Torah which states that the unclean must be purified. Some people, however, could not be purified. The frail, lame, sick, blind, and infirmed were forbidden from entering the Temple. Those were the people to whom Jesus ministered, those with an oppressed spirit. Jesus seemed to care for the outcasts and those excluded from society and even religion. Jesus desired to bring every person salvation.

Jesus gave hope to the hopeless and power to the powerless by giving them a way to control their lives and feel contentment. He brought them all the things they did not have in this life: hope, freedom, joy, power, and strength. The summary of Jesus' life was given by Peter in Acts 10:38, "He went about doing good."

Huston Smith described being around Jesus in the following way:

"The people who first heard Jesus' disciples proclaiming the Good News were as impressed by what they saw as what they heard. They saw lives transformed-men and women who were ordinary in every way except for the fact that they seemed to have found the secret of living. They evidenced a

*tranquility, a simplicity, and cheerfulness that
their hearers had nowhere else encountered.
Here were people who seemed to be making a
success of the enterprise everyone would like
to succeed at-that of life itself."[13]*

In the 1995 movie *Three Wishes* Patrick Swayze
plays a mysterious man who becomes part of a
family and ends up granting a wish to each family
member. Many years later, when he sees the little
boy in the family (who has since become a man),
the man complains that he had never gotten his wish.
Patrick Swayze told him, "You were always wishing
for what you didn't have; my wish for you was that
you find happiness in whatever you had." That desire
for us to find accomplishment in the life we have
sounds very much like Jesus' wish for his disciples
to find peace through God.

Jesus' message was to use the resources that
exist to provide care for all people. Jesus spent years
preaching and living out his message to create an
egalitarian and democratic society. He invited people
to love one another, to share their wealth, and to see
that their gift to each other was their service to each
other. Jesus' goal for community was equal political,
social, economic, and civil power where an undiffer-
entiated and classless community shared resources
for the benefit of all.

Jesus Christ did not preach about or model
retribution, payback or the use of force. He never
advocated killing, even of murderers. Jesus didn't
attempt to inflict pain. He did not want people to

feel sadness, but joy. He allowed people to make their own decisions. He never coerced, he invited. He showed his power not through force but in the strength of love. Jesus didn't exact revenge. When he rose from the dead, he didn't storm into the Temple and shout, "You picked on the wrong man!" Following Gods will does not provide for the justification of evil, but God's name has often been and is still used to justify evil in the Middle East and throughout the world as suicide bombers and global terrorists seek to impose their will.

No individual should feel detached, hopeless, and totally depressed in a relationship with God. In *Jesus*, E. Schillebeeckx wrote, "Being sad in Jesus' presence (was) an existential impossibility."[14] Jesus told his disciples that his teachings were to this end: "That my joy may be in you, and your joy may be complete." (John 15:11) Jesus' concern was not death, but life. "I am come that they might have life, and that they might have it more abundantly" (John 10:10).

The book *The DaVinci Papers* by Dan Brown, theorizes about a secret society of the Catholic Church supposedly entrusted with protecting the interests of the institutional church throughout the middle ages which even resorted to murder to protect the Churches secrets. Questions raised by the book and the possibility of these speculations being true has many Catholics questioning their faith, but why should it matter to us if Jesus had brothers and sisters or whether Jesus and Mary Magdalene were actually married?

If the message of Jesus' life is not compromised by facts regarding his family then maybe we should focus more on his message of love and his divinity rather than being concerned with what his favorite color was, whether he was married or not, or if he had brothers and sisters. Our concern should be what God wants from us and what we can do to get closer to God.

Sacrifice

Early man did not know how to explain what the sun was, why the sun came up every day or why rain came. Whatever could not be controlled or explained was attributed to higher powers or gods, and man attempted to placate these gods. Often the youngest and most able-bodied humans were sacrificed to make the gods happy. The gods were "paid off" just as extortionists receive blackmail. As time went on, in place of human sacrifice, man offered animals and the first harvest of crops as a form of sacrifice to the gods. The whole idea of sacrifice was based on keeping the gods satisfied by giving them what was most important and valuable.

Jesus explained what we can offer as sacrifice to God: our time and faith. Hosea 6:5 - 6 says, "What I want from you is plain and clear: I want your constant love, not your animal sacrifices. I would rather have people know me than have them burn offerings to me." And in Matthew 9:13: "Go out and find what is meant by the scripture that says: 'It is kindness that I want, not animal sacrifices.'" It seems what God wants from us is the "best" of ourselves that we can offer. It seems that the sacrifice God wants, is us.

Jesus taught us to stop imposing our will and to offer ourselves in service to others to help them acquire food, clothing and shelter to survive. We are asked to be unselfish enough to consider God's concerns instead of our own so that God can work through us as we attend to the needs of others. Jesus said that God does not want to be close to us or around us; God wants to be one with us, a part of our lives, within us.

God is the answer to our spiritual hunger and our desire to know why we exist. Jesus told his disciples that he was the bread of life. He said whoever ate of his bread would have eternal life. When the ancient Jews, Egyptian and Arabian peoples who lived around the Mediterranean region would make animal sacrifices, they would eat the flesh of the animal but they would not have anything to do with the blood. Blood was associated with the life of the animal.

Jesus invited people to eat his body and drink his blood. That would make him part of them. The gospel says many people were disgusted by what Jesus said and left Jesus' company because of such a revolting idea, but it should be obvious to us today that Jesus was not espousing cannibalism but making a symbolic point about our absolute oneness with God.

Jesus message was not that God be apart *from* our lives, but that God be part *of* our lives. We are not divorced parents with visitation rights to God only on the weekend; we have access to our relationship with God 24 hours a day, seven days a week, like the single parent of a newborn baby who has sole custody. Jesus was attempting to raise the awareness of his listeners and clarify the personal relationship that existed between them and God. Our relationship with God must be a personal one. God is not their God; God is our God, personally.

What we need for our survival are air, food, and water. Jesus refers to himself as the bread of life and claims he can provide water so we will never be thirsty. To ancient peoples clean water was essential for survival, and bread, which was one of the only foods available to eat, was the staple of their diet; even being called the "staff of life." To breathe means to inspire. Jesus taught that God can be the spirit which gives us life, our inspiration, our very breath. Jesus explained where God wants to be in relation to us: in our every breath, our inspiration, the source of our life and essential for us to survive.

CHAPTER SEVEN

What is God's message and how do we deliver it?

Jesus' message was love. Christ asked us to love others not as we love our imperfect selves but as God has loved us, warts and all. The Persian poet Kahlil Gibran wrote, "When you love you should not say, 'God is in my heart ' but rather 'I am in the heart of God.' And think not that you can direct the course of love, for love, if it finds you worthy, directs your course."[15] Our journey to God is through the love Jesus spoke of. What Jesus means by love is famously described in Corinthians 1 13:1 - 8:

> *If I speak in human and angelic tongues*
> *but do not have love, I am a resounding gong*
> *or a clashing cymbal. And if I have the gift of*
> *prophesy and comprehend all mysteries and*
> *all knowledge; if I have faith enough to move*

mountains but do not have love, I am nothing. If I give away everything I own and if I hand over my body so that I may boast, but do not have love, I gain nothing.

Love is patient, love is kind. It is not jealous, it is not pompous, it is not inflated, it is not rude, it does not seek its own interests, it is not quick-tempered, it does not brood over injury, it does not rejoice over wrong-doing but rejoices with the truth. It bears all things, believes all things, hopes all things, endures all things. Love never fails.

People who believe in Jesus as God's messenger see a God of love who has given us the power of our free will and choice. Since God is love, replace "love" with "God" in the scripture reading above to see the beautiful imagery of God. God seems to come into focus when we define God in terms of love:

If I speak in human and angelic tongues but do not have God, I am a resounding gong or a clashing cymbal. And if I have the gift of prophesy and comprehend all mysteries and all knowledge; if I have faith enough to move mountains but do not have God, I am nothing. If I give away everything I own and if I hand over my body so that I may boast, but do not have God, I gain nothing.

God is patient, God is kind. God is not jealous, pompous, inflated, or rude, God does not seek selfish interests, is not quick-tempered, does not brood over injury, does not rejoice over wrongdoing but rejoices in the truth. God bears all things, believes all things, hopes all things, endures all things. God never fails.

God wants us to be able to put ourselves into the reading where we see the word love. What love is, God is; they are one and the same. Christians strive to be one with God and embody love. If we are disciples of Jesus, our goal is to be more like Jesus and wherever we see love and God, we should be able to put ourselves.

Can we put ourselves in the reading where we see the word love? Do we reflect all (or any) of those ideals? Comparing ourselves to love and God should make clear to us what we have to do and how we should act to become practicing Christians. As we collect our trophies, we should stop to remember Jesus and make our accomplishments in terms of love.

Love is both a noun and a verb. Love heals, love renews, and love brings us closer to God. Deepak Chopra in *The Path to Love* writes, "The spiritual meaning of love is measured by what it can do."[16] Love is not something we *feel* but something we *do*. Our relationship with our Lord involves other people because the goal of Christianity is to bring into the world the kingdom of shared mutual concern expressed through love.

Thousands of years ago, people's fear of God prevented them from feeling anything but persecuted under the constant, watchful eye of a judgmental, power-wielding enforcer. The God written about in the Old Testament dispenses some hard justice and demands complete allegiance. The God whom Jesus spoke of allows us to choose, offering the truth that if we allow God to help us live our life, we will benefit, not only by finding meaning for our existence but also by attaining the trophy, the accomplishment, the reward of eternal life and salvation.

Real Wealth

Jesus can provide us with God's perspective of wealth. An anonymous author once wrote, "If you want to feel rich, just count all of the things you have that money can't buy." We all want more money, and we imagine that wealth would change our lives completely, bring us an enormous reduction in stress and pressure, and make us satisfied. We all want a fantasy vacation and we all need to take a break from our schedule, but is luxury the trophy we pursue? Imagine what it would be like to have unlimited wealth and be able to afford a vacation lifestyle every day.

Let's say that you wake up at the beach, in the mountains or wherever you would love to be in a massive bed in a beautiful room. Sleep until noon if you like. You have no schedule, so you can lounge around and have a casual breakfast or a formal gourmet meal. Your day is spent doing nothing or doing what you want: shopping, golfing, visiting sights, you decide over a sumptuous lunch. This brings you to dinner, where you can consume as much of your favorite food and drink as you want. Your schedule is what you want it to be. When you get to bed, you have spent the entire day doing only what you have wanted to do.

Now imagine having the same schedule for a few more days, weeks, even a few months. If that is really how we want to live until we die, we don't want anything from God; all we want is self-indulgence, which God does not provide. As we strive to improve our physical comfort, we should remember that Jesus was never concerned with the status and possessions people had but how close they were to God. In Mark 10:17 - 27 we read:

> *As Jesus was setting out on a journey, a man ran up, knelt down before him, and asked him, "Good teacher, what must I do to inherit eternal life?" Jesus answered him, "You know the commandments: You shall not kill, you shall not commit adultery; you shall not steal; you shall not bear false witness; you shall not defraud; honor your father and your mother."*
>
> *He replied and said to him, "Teacher, all of these I have observed from my youth." Jesus, looking at him, loved him and said to him, "You are lacking in one thing. Go, sell what you have, and give to the poor and you will have treasure in heaven; then come, follow me." At that statement his face fell, and he went away sad, for he had many possessions.*

> *Jesus looked around and said to his disciples, "How hard it is for those who have wealth to enter the kingdom of God!" The disciples were amazed at his words. So Jesus again said to them in reply, "Children how hard it is to enter the kingdom of God! It is easier for a camel to pass through the eye of a needle than for one who is rich to enter the kingdom of God." They were exceedingly astonished and said among themselves, "Then who can be saved?" Jesus looked at them and said, "For human beings it is impossible, but not for God. All things are possible for God."*

Jesus never asks about the wealth of the man, only how he can aid the needy. It was not a directive for everyone to give away whatever they owned. Jesus' warning was about the dangers of wealth and how it may come between us and God. No individual or institution should come between us and God, even ones that may impose obligations on us. Our relationship with God should be the one most important thing in our lives.

Luke 14:26 contains this shocking statement from Jesus: "If anyone comes to me without hating his father and mother, wife and children, brothers and sisters, and even his own life, he cannot be my disciple." These words do not mean we should hate those closest to us, which is totally contrary to what Jesus preached. Jesus probably meant that nothing in our lives should come between us and God. Other translations change the passage to say, "If anyone comes to me without loving me more than his mother and father, he cannot be my disciple," which is more consistent with Jesus' teachings.

Jesus reminded them that they might possibly have to sacrifice getting along with some people, including their own church or family, to keep God as the central focus of their lives. When the statement was made, Jesus was speaking to a great crowd who expected him to lead them by way of force like an earthly king. He was making clear what discipleship really meant.

This warning is for us, too. It warns us about the danger of allowing ourselves to be distracted from God by popularity, wealth, fame, influence, and pride, all the trappings of a "successful" modern life. God must be the central wealth of our lives even if this means simplifying our lives and eschewing the trappings of material comfort.

God wants nothing more than to show us how to make our lives so full we are bursting with enthusiasm. The really great news is that this is a free offer and all we have to do is respond. Luke 16:19-30 tells us:

> *There was a rich man who was dressed in purple garments and fine linens and dined sumptuously every day. And lying at his door was a poor man named Lazarus, covered with sores, who would gladly have eaten the scraps that fell from the rich man's table.*
> *Dogs even used to come and lick his sores. When the poor man died, he was carried away*

by angels to the bosom of Abraham. The rich man also died and was buried, and from the netherworld, where he was in torment, he raised his eyes and saw Abraham far off and Lazarus at his side. And he cried out, "Father Abraham, have pity on me. Send Lazarus to dip the tip of his finger in water and cool my tongue, for I am suffering torment in these flames."

Abraham replied, "My child, remember that you received what was good during your lifetime while Lazarus likewise received what was bad; but now he is comforted here, whereas you are tormented. Moreover, between us and you a great chasm is established to prevent anyone from crossing who might wish to cross from our side to yours or from your side to ours." He said, "Then I beg you, father, send him to my father's house, for I have five brothers, so that he may warn them, lest they too come to this place of torment." But Abraham replied, "They have Moses and the prophets. Let them listen to them." He said, "Oh no, father Abraham, but if someone from the dead goes to them, they will repent." Then Abraham said, "If they will not listen to Moses and the prophets, neither will they be persuaded if someone should rise from the dead."

On hearing this, the Pharisees would have been shocked because popular belief in Jesus' day equated wealth and status with favor from God. When wealth blinds us to the people in need right at our door, our wealth is coming between us and God. Jesus taught us to be connected to each other, but our tendency in society is to use wealth to separate ourselves from others. That's why today we have private social or country clubs, first class, preferential seating, luxury suites, and gated communities.

The wealth God provides is not necessarily the luxury of physical comfort. Think about trying to get a gift for the richest woman in the world. We certainly couldn't give her anything monetary, so what could we give her? What could we possibly get her that she couldn't go out and buy for herself? Probably nothing, but God can provide her some extremely valuable gifts that no amount of money can buy: hope and forgiveness, joy and peace.

Only we know whether we can live without what we own. Jesus spread a message of extreme service. Jesus even said, "What good is it for a man to gain the whole world if he loses his soul?" What good is it for us to accumulate incredible wealth if we are not happy and do not feel good about our lives? Our pursuit of possessions might keep us from doing God's work and our personal comfort and pursuit of luxury might blind us to the needs of the poor around us. Our pursuit of luxury might also not bring us the satisfaction we want in our lives, as the poem Richard Cory by Edwin Arlington Robinson shows:

Whenever Richard Cory went down town,
We people on the pavement looked at him;

He was a gentleman from sole to crown,
Clean favored, and imperially slim.
And he was always quietly arrayed,
And he was always human when he talked;
But still he fluttered pulses when he said,
"Good-morning" and he glittered when he
*   walked.*
And he was rich-yes, richer than a king-
And admirably schooled in every grace;
In fine we thought that he was everything
To make us wish that we were in his place.
So on we worked, and waited for the light,
And went without the meat, and cursed the
*   bread;*
And Richard Cory, one calm summer night,
Went home and put a bullet through his head.

Richard Cory obviously never found what he was looking for, even in his possessions and status. Only God can provide us with the inner wealth of the joy of life.

Luxury is about the outside of our lives; how we feel about ourselves on the inside is what brings us joy. That's why Jesus Christ's message appealed to people two thousand years ago and why it might appeal to us today. An all expense-paid vacation or a million dollars might not bring us the fulfillment we want to feel on the inside. What Jesus Christ spoke of was the one thing people without any means or worldly possessions could attain and the one thing those with the means to obtain any worldly possession could not buy. The comfort God provides is not necessarily physical comfort but emotional comfort.

Poor people can be happy with their lives knowing that they are loved, they are loveable and capable of loving, and be satisfied through God's peace. Just as the outcasts of society in Jesus' time found their treasure inside their hearts, we can do the same and approach and appreciate each moment as though we'll never have another one just like it. When we do that, we can spend our time not in pursuit of possessions but in pursuit of the bread, water, and air of God. The "good life" everyone speaks about is being aware and experiencing the wealth of God right here with us.

Deciding to "Put on Christ" or use God as the measure of our accomplishments gives our lives tremendous possibilities and allows us to recognize that our lives are gifts from God. Buying a jersey of a professional athlete such as Michael Jordan, Michael Vick or Barry Bonds means we love how they play and want to be like them, but no one is going to mistake us for any one of them. Putting on Christ is like putting on Jesus' jersey so that people can see us attempting to act like Jesus through how we show compassion and concern. A practicing Catholic or Christian is a person who is acting as Jesus taught.

CHAPTER EIGHT

The Road to God is Straight and Narrow

Christianity is based on a God with a forgiving nature, and it is lucky for us imperfect humans that our creator is benevolent. Messengers of God have always been imperfect, that's why Jesus forgave sins and why God's forgiveness is available: because we are all sinners. What remains is Jesus' perfect message and imperfect messengers to deliver it. We are all sinners but if we believe we are not worthy of God's blessings because we are flawed, we are giving up and giving in to sin, putting all the responsibility for our lives on God, making it much more difficult for God to work through us.

Therefore, should any Christian not living a sinless life be called a hypocrite? No, because a hypocrite is a fraud. We are simply sinners unless we purposely mislead others and misrepresent ourselves; humans are imperfect as a matter of fact, but it was Jesus himself who said, "The last shall be first and the first shall be last." This is the opposite of our "winning is everything" trophy case mentality and it should help us clarify the nature of the Christian God.

Any man of God and faith who is found to have had an affair or child out of wedlock, done drugs, been a pedophile, or sinned in some way may be a hypocrite, but he or she is also human. For all of us sinful humans, God has made available what may be the most comforting fact of our existence: the opportunity to change and be forgiven for our failings; redemption.

We're all Sinners

Some Christians abuse drugs, while others abuse their spouses or their children. Some Christians are unfaithful to their spouses while some Christian businessmen cheat, lie, and steal. Christians use internet pornography and some make and sell pornography. There are murderers sitting in church. There are many kinds of abuse, and Christians are involved in all forms of it. If we make a show of our religion by putting our "I love Jesus" bumper sticker on our car and treat people badly, we are misrepresenting ourselves and our religion.

Every individual and institution is flawed. We're all imperfect and that's what makes being honest so difficult, but that fact makes God's perfection clearer. We're all in the same boat and all have a right to feel inadequate. Since we all have faults, it's easy to make fun of people. All we have to do is point them out. Arrogance is a facade; we're all vulnerable. If everyone knew everything we have done and everything we think, we could be embarrassed and unsure of their acceptance. It's much harder to allow people to be human and to try to make people feel good about themselves than ridicule their faults. In John 8: 3 - 11 it is written:

> *Then the scribes brought a woman who had been caught in adultery and made her stand in the middle. They said to him, "Teacher, this woman was caught in the very act of committing adultery. Now in the law, Moses commanded us to stone such women. So what do you say?" They said this to test him, so that they could have some charge to bring against him. Jesus bent down and began to write on the ground with his finger. But when they continued asking him, he straightened up and said to them, "Let the one among you who is without sin be the first to throw a stone at her."*
>
> *Again he bent down and wrote on the ground. And in response, they went away one by one, beginning with the elders. So he was left alone with the woman before him. Then Jesus straightened up and said to her, "Woman, where are they? Has no one condemned you?" She replied, "No one, sir." Then Jesus said, "Neither do I condemn you. Go, and from now on do not sin anymore."*

If we ever need assurance and comfort that we have God's support, all we need to do is think about the adulterous woman and how much she represents us. The woman was a sinner, but Jesus didn't condemn her. He forgave her and allowed her to begin again. Just as Jesus intervened when people were about to kill the woman, God gives us the chance to start over and be forgiven for our sins. She didn't even expect or ask for forgiveness and we don't know if she repented, Jesus simply gave her the opportunity to begin again.

God forgives us and tells us to sin no more. When we sin, we first need to admit our wrong, forgive ourselves and vow to sin no more and move on with our lives. "Sin" means literally to miss the mark, as when we shoot an arrow at a target. The Jewish service for Yom Kippur addresses this. Ten days after the celebration of the Jewish New Year, the "day of atonement" is a day of worship and fasting where Jews forgive each others sins as God forgives them. When we miss the target of God, we harm ourselves, not God. The strongest reason for not continuing to sin is sin keeps us from getting closer to God. Sin hurts us, not God.

God will always be with us with unfailing, unconditional acceptance and will always come to our defense and give us another chance if we are honestly repentant. God is the source of our forgiveness. If we are truly sorry and swear to improve our behavior, God will allow us to start over. Jesus said, "As far as the east is from the west, so far have I put your past transgressions from you." The God of

Christianity offers us hope in spite of our imperfections and allows us to concentrate on attaining wealth from God's perspective.

Sampling God: The Trial Size

What if God were the best food that we had never eaten or the best book that we had never read? What if God were the best movie ever made, the most beautiful music ever written, or the nicest person in the world we had never seen, heard, or met? What if God could make us feel as though we just won a big trophy? To find the God that theologians and religions speak about, the first step of our journey is to become open to what God can bring to our lives and be willing to test God out.

If we don't want anything and we don't need anything, we won't look for anything. If we're feeling healthy, we usually won't go see a doctor. Similarly, there's no reason for us to seek God unless something is missing from our lives or we're curious about what God could bring us. We may have to want or lack something before we decide to seek God and try to make a place for God in our lives.

We make New Year's resolutions, birthday wishes, and Lenten sacrifices, we join diet plans and fitness regimens constantly attempting to "get our act together" and straighten up our lives. But, as with most resolutions, we fail and end up right back where we started. Justin vowed to lose weight every New Years for the last 10 years.

Each year after dieting for several weeks he not only gained back his weight, but some additional weight so after a decade he was no closer to his goal and even more overweight, so he finally joined a weight-loss club. Similarly, we need help to find God. If achieving our wishes were as simple as saying so, and if we could succeed all by ourselves, we would never fail and we wouldn't need help.

Just as we tend to appreciate something after we lose it, we tend to look for God when we're forced to in hopeless situations or trying times. Soldiers in foxholes and people in crisis often pray and make a deal with God in a life threatening situation. Oswald Chambers wrote, "When a man is at his wits end it is not a cowardly thing to pray, it is the only way he can get in touch with reality." When we can't accomplish a task by ourselves, we give God a chance by asking God and pleading. Regardless of the circumstances, the important thing is our desire to find out more about God.

As little children we must be fed because we can't feed ourselves. Our parents may have taken us to Sunday mass every week while we were growing up. Many private school children are forced to attend church every week while they live with their parents, but as soon as they leave home, they stop attending church because they have no connection to their faith. We need to be told about God initially, but until we experience God for ourselves, we have no true connection and our beliefs may amount to myth.

Parents and friends may have good intentions when they "feed us" or bring us up according to their religious perspectives when we're young. A child may feel a connection to God without knowing what the feeling is. Hopefully, religion can help explain to the child just what he is feeling but the experience is personal.

We use religion to get a better concept of our relationship with God but our religion is not an obligation but a choice. Our faith and God belong to us, not our mother, our minister, or the Holy Father the Pope. Our desire to get closer to God cannot come externally from the church, our parents, or our friends but only from inside of us.

We are taught that attending mass, praying, giving money to the church and deference to those in authority in the church will result in a closer personal relationship with God. If we say we're hungry, we can expect God and religions to feed us our spiritual food, but we then end up depending on the church to provide for us like a caterer for our next meal.

If a woman comes to us every day and gives us a piece of bread, we rely on her for our food. We can rely on the church to provide our relationship with God for us. In our relationship with the church, we must make sure the church provides us with the knowledge and materials to learn how to cook for ourselves and make our own bread. We are the individuals who are hungry and we must develop our own personal relationship with God. The church is the culinary school where we who are hungry can learn the recipe to prepare our own relationship with God.

Being told about how God is important and how we'll love God, religion, and spirituality is like going out to eat with a well-meaning friend who keeps telling us, "Get the sweet and sour chicken, you'll love it." They mean well, but ultimately we have to find out for ourselves what we like. Only after tasting a certain food for ourselves can we truly understand what it tastes like and if we like it. In the same way, we can have a personal opinion about God only by experiencing God for ourselves. In the same way we have our own connection to God; we decide what we eat and how much we eat.

Religion and the church are like museums we visit to find out about God and learn about all the unknowns of life, but we can leave Church feeling there's nothing of ours in there. Like seeing a beautiful painting or an exotic luxury car, we appreciate what we see but we also feel the item doesn't belong to us. If our faith and relationship with God are things we only have based on what other people tell us we will use them and give them back feeling emotionally detached from them because they are not ours. We fail to realize we own everything we see.

Our Christian faith is not the Catholic, Lutheran, Episcopalian, or Mormon Church institution, it is *ours*. Jesus died to rescue *us*. The only place where God can truly exist in this world is in this moment and in our heart. When we see God as our personal savior we are not passive in receiving information about God but active in obtaining information and we replace our religious myths and superstitions with reality.

In our search for meaning do we ever consider the possibility that we ourselves are important?

Ownership of our relationship with God is the most critical awareness of our lives. Through our personal decisions we decide how much we allow God into our lives. We must make the God which religions speak of our personal God. Through discovering ourselves we find what God can bring to our lives, and realize why we seek God: to find out more about ourselves.

William Inge wrote, "Prayer gives a man the opportunity of getting to know a gentleman he hardly ever meets. I do not mean his maker, but himself." T.T. Munger wrote: "Knowledge and personality make doubt possible, but knowledge is also the cure of doubt; and when we get a full and adequate sense of personality we are lifted into a region where doubt is almost impossible, for no man can know himself as he is, and the fullness of his nature, without also knowing God."

Not relying on our own experience is like believing rumors about someone. Being told God is mean and vengeful, or merciful and compassionate may cause us to prejudge God. We can use what we hear as a warning to be cautious or we can evaluate God based on our personal interaction. We hope people judge us by how we treat them rather than prejudge us based on what they hear about us; shouldn't we extend the same courtesy to God?

Getting to heaven by Association

Religion may help us with our awareness of God, but if we think we're going to win because we went to mass or prayed to God before the game; if we assume we are getting to Heaven because we're a Lutheran, Mormon, Catholic, Jew, or Muslim we may be fooling ourselves. If we believe we are saved because we are a nun, priest, rabbi, minister or member of a certain faith then nothing is required of us and we have no personal responsibility: our membership will save us.

Being a part of a bigger whole, such as a certain religious denomination, connects us to others but it does not guarantee anything. It can make us a passive spectator and lead us to want to take credit for what other people accomplish. We may become the number one fan of a sports team, show allegiance to our college, and wear our ethnic heritage with pride like a badge. We may expect a personal reward when our favorite team wins the Super Bowl or World Series, we may align ourselves with Democratic or Republican political ideology or simply try to bolster our own status with our religious affiliation. That may lead us to want what is not really ours by taking credit for our allegiance.

While attending West Virginia University years ago, an undergraduate was hitchhiking between the school's downtown campus and Evansdale campus when he was picked up by a driver. He shook hands, introduced himself, and thanked the man for picking him up.

The man said, "I recognize your name. Aren't you the editor of the school paper?"

"No," the hitchhiker replied, "that's my brother."

"Aren't you the news anchor on that WVU tele-vision station?" the driver inquired again.

"No, that's my sister."

"Oh, you're the President of the rugby club."

"No," the rider laughed. "That's my cousin; I'm nobody."

The undergrad realized that no matter how closely related he was to other people, his identity was based solely on what he did personally. God does not have a line on our application for Heaven that asks for religious affiliation, accomplishments in terms of our celebrity status, corporate leaders we know or even political rallies or state dinners we have attended. God doesn't count our trophies. No organized religion has the right membership card to get any of us into heaven, and our vouchers are not transferable. If heaven is our reward then God is the talent scout.

Heaven is not for members of one team only but for the All-Star team, the best players in God's game. God will not judge us based on what team we play for but how well we love; not because we call ourselves Christians but because of our Christian deeds. We're not on the team just because we wear the uniform, and we shouldn't feel like a part of the team unless we get to play and contribute. We stand all by ourselves and give an account of our lives to enter heaven; no one else can do it for us. A beggar wearing a designer suit is still poor. A church-goer who is only fulfilling a religious obligation without feeling any connection to God inside is still spiritually poor.

Our actions matter more than our religious affiliation. We can be involved in a relationship with God and belong to an organized religion for two very different reasons: for appearance or utility. The teaching of Islam, to "Love the pitcher less, and the water more," reminds us to pay more attention to God, the function of our lives, rather than the form we follow and the package God comes in.

Religion can be like body-building. We can lift weights to enhance the way we look to others, or we can lift weights to develop strength that we can use for utility and function. We can belong to a church so others will see us belong, or so we can put our connection to the Lord into practice to find meaning in our lives.

CHAPTER NINE

Making their God our God

Today, religious doctrine can be confusing. Theologians, ministers, priests, clerics, preachers and representatives of religions all attempt to explain God's plan to us, but if there are so many different religions and they can't agree on an explanation of God, how can we hope to understand God? There is so much information many of us may feel as if we are trying to interpret a legal document. Because we can feel unqualified to interpret religion we may stay away from God. We should be wary of any faith or institution claiming to tell us what God wants. We must work through our own uncertainty and doubt by experiencing God for ourselves. God is our personal savior.

Sophy Burnham wrote: "To believe in God or in a guiding force because someone tells you to is the height of stupidity. We are given senses to receive our information within. With our own eyes we see, and with our own skin we feel. With our intelligence, it is intended that we understand. But each person must puzzle it out for himself or herself."

We cannot be forced to get closer to God by attendance at mass or religious services but we must accept the invitation ourselves. To have a closer relationship with God, we should be focusing on what we can do to internalize God more rather than obsessing over what obligations we have, such as attending mass, or what we should avoid, such as not eating meat on Friday during Lent.

Personalizing a relationship with God is like moving from a rented or subsidized apartment into a home that we own. Things immediately change. We take more care of a house or car that we own. Renting a house or car usually leads us to worry more about how we can avoid damaging it than caring for it.

We pay more attention to a house that we own and we become actively involved in maintaining and improving it. Our relationship with God is something we own, not something that we rent or borrow from someone else. If we own our relationship with God we will take care of it, nurture it and try to make it better. We will fix it up because it is ours.

Separating God from the institution

If we allow the church or anyone else to form our idea of how we contact God, we are cheating ourselves of our own spirituality. If we do not arrive at our own individual concept of who God is, we can follow the individuals and masses throughout history from Adolph Hitler to Osama Bin Laden, who rationalized all types of evil by invoking the name of God.

If we don't feel what God brings to our lives, we can end up going through the motions of ritual for no apparent reason. We can become a church-goer, not necessarily a believer, depending on other people or the church to provide us with salvation simply by belonging to a church or congregation and attempt to get credit for our associations.

Wisdom and knowledge are gained through learning how to incorporate the information we know into our own lives, often through experience. We may know about God's wisdom, but the point is to find out how to use and apply God's message. How can this vague, abstract material be made more concrete and accessible?

Just like in school, by personalizing the material and applying what we know to our daily life, not simply by following the rules and procedures. God is not religion, and unless we separate God from the institutional church, we may not recognize the personal ownership of our relationship with God. Institutions do not have God's unlisted phone number and contact God for us; we contact God ourselves.

In school, we receive top grade if we do an excellent job of learning the material presented to us in class, but we are passive receivers of what is presented. Someone else decides all the questions and what is important for us to know. Our grade means that we accomplished what we were supposed to, but we might never apply what we learned to our lives.

In seventh grade at school, Cara gets bored when she loses sight of the meaning of her studies. She asks, "When am I ever going to use this information?" Cara ends up memorizing material which means nothing to her and forgetting it right after the final exam. She hasn't learned any information she can use.

When Cara hears about God from ministers, priests, and people who claim to be speaking for God, she asks herself, "What does all this have to do with me personally? Religious authorities constantly tell Cara: "This is what God is like and this is what God wants you to do!" Do they really know what God wants her to do, or are they just giving her their opinion as if they are telling her what food she'll love at a certain restaurant?

In school we compile facts and collect information but until we find a way to use and apply it the information remains without personal significance to us and may not be effective in helping us. Love and the love of God can be learned intellectually, but we can relate to love only when our personal experience makes it real. When we write the questions ourselves we get a better idea of what we learn and how it relates to our life.

Relationships

Our relationships can and should reflect who we are, including the relationship we have between the seen world and the unseen world, the known and the unknown, and what is visible and what is intuited or felt. Our lives will be defined by the relationships we have with ourselves, God, religion and other people. Our lives will also be defined by our connection to all the facets of our daily existence, including alcohol, sex, drugs, food, material items, money, wealth, fame, popularity, power, and influence.

We are often taught to fear punishment as "payback" for our actions because belief can cause fear by superstition. Rosie O'Donnell told the editor of her magazine, *Rosie*, that "People who lie, get cancer" when she was fighting with the woman simply to inflict pain and cause fear. We are taught that if we don't follow the rules, somehow God will see us unfit or unworthy of saving. We might be afraid of God because we are told by our minister that if we drink alcohol we'll go to hell and eternal damnation, or because a Nun threatens us with God's punishment if we acknowledge our sexuality and the temptations it brings.

As we grow up, we all wish we had better relationships with those around us. In school the most popular kids are the envy of everyone else in class. Insecurity and fear of rejection are enormous burdens we bear. We will do what we have to for love and self-acceptance. We all want to feel good and we try to do so through our associations and relationships with the people in our lives. But if we can't love and accept who we are and feel comfortable with ourselves we can never get past our own self absorption and quest for validation.

A young girl with a poor self-image may use sex for acceptance, seeing that the boys pay attention to her if she is promiscuous. A boy with feelings of depression may use drugs to take away his feelings of insecurity or deaden his pain. The obese child who becomes the class clown hides behind the mask of indifference to conceal his own sadness and depression.

We all search for meaning in our lives through our relationships. If we define the supreme power in the universe and attempt to improve our relationship with God; every single thing we do should bring us closer to that God. We might believe God is a predator and we are the prey as if God is "out to get us" hiding in wait to catch us doing wrong and make us pay for our mistakes to cause us suffering. If we see God as the angry, jealous, ruthless punisher found in the Old Testament we might live attempting to hide from God and we might live our whole life in fear and dread.

The comic strip Calvin and Hobbes by Bill Waterson featured one strip in which Calvin, a little boy, was lying on a hillside with his "living" stuffed tiger, Hobbes. Hobbes asked Calvin if he believed in God, and Calvin responded, "Well, *some*body's out to get me." The Christian God is a god of love and joy. We should come to the realization that God *is* out to "get us" but not in the way we fear. God is attempting to pick us up and help us to find Heaven and Salvation.

Covenant Signing: Individuals Only

People or organizations may help us find God, but the promise of salvation is made to us individually and we are personally responsible for entering an agreement with God through our individual actions. A covenant is a special agreement, pledge, and promise, and we have just such a contract from God. We can either sign or not, but the contract, our covenant, is always there. Our personal association with God is not an association with a religion. The contract is not between institutions and God and it is not attained through association. It is ours to sign personally.

The church does not dole out God or grace in portions dependant on how much money we contribute. Religions do not have the recipe for making faith, but we do. We can ignore, isolate, neglect, or disown God and treat God like an acquaintance or a distant relative as people do with family members whom they find embarrassing. We can even pretend God isn't there, but like it or not we are related to our creator.

As our relative, God can take many forms: the judgmental father we run to for forgiveness and approval; the mother we seek for comfort; the doting grandparent, the mean, detached "Dutch Uncle" who spies on us and punishes us, the step-parent who we never really feel close to, or the person who is not related to us but we call "Aunt" or "Uncle" anyway. God can also literally be our soul mate and closest friend. We must recognize which relative God is for us, consider what relative we are to God and decide whether we want to change that existing relationship.

Our relationship with God falls somewhere among the following possibilities or categories:

1. Welfare Recipients passively wait to receive what God gives them as a handout. Inactive, relegated to taking but giving nothing to God they are not personally involved in any way but hold out hope for being given an inheritance or winning the lottery. Welfare Recipients acknowledge God "just in case" if at all, view God as the ultimate trophy-giver and possess a "you take care of me" attitude.

2. Businesspeople.

2A. Negotiators adhere to the letter of the law. Hagglers, bargainers, barterers, and traders say, "I'll do something for you if you do something for me." Maybe they will go to Christmas and Easter services to satisfy religious requirements. They believe God owes them something good in return for every good act they do and they expect to be punished by God for every failure or omission on their part. They are big believers in trophies from God and what they receive is nothing personal, it's strictly business.

   They want to negotiate their spiritual and humanitarian obligations. They want to do less than whatever is required. They say, "How much do I have to do?" and "I'm not doing all *that*." They are faithful only up to the point where they begin to feel discomfort.

2B Vendors sell God and grace in any faith. This category is not for clerics only, but also for any overbearing disciple who sells us what God wants. They tell us what to do to *earn* God. They tell us that grace, favor, blessings, good luck, wealth, happiness, and heaven are all things we earn, not achieve. They are pushy, high-pressure salespeople who depend on force and guilt to get their way.

They operate like a fortuneteller, preying on all who allow the superstition and myth of procedure to enter the relationship between God and the individual. They add hoops for us to jump through. The televangelist who solicits money to continue his ministry and to pray for the television viewer is one example. People not in organized religion see all religions and churches as being in this category, existing solely to take advantage of people and be God's broker or agent.

3. Mass Consumers (no pun intended) are those believers who are aligned with their religion from birth and attend services because that's what they are supposed to do. Their relationship with God has never been examined and their religious affiliation is akin to being a member of a club even though they feel nothing personally.

They look like a Christian in that their outfit and demeanor are that of a Christian, but they have no personal attachment or connection to God or the church. They act merely out of habit, a sense of obligation, or a desire to make an impression. Their relationship with God has always been defined for them in other peoples terms. They are simply going through the motions like a robot carrying out a perceived order. A mannequin could stand in for them if necessary. They do not negotiate because they have no expectations.

4. Dissatisfied customers are unhappy with or have problems with either the Vendors, or God, pointing out the imperfections or failures of both. They are critics who review every tragedy, senseless killing, and malevolent act by saying, "How could a God allow these terrible things to happen?" Claims of God's intercession in our lives are met with the response, "Prove it," or "Show me."

These individuals love to be the ultimate judges of reality and regard obligation and commitment with a "We'll see" attitude. They act only when convenient to them and expect God to perform like a genie or magician. They are skeptics filled with doubt and question everything. While they are involved in religion through grudging acknowledgment, they are contrary and impossible to please. While they are testing institutional religion and theology by questioning everything, they cultivate a spirit of opposition for its own sake. Such a combative stance rarely results in growth and learning.

5   Shoppers

5A.   Bargain hunters explore all the options and choices, looking for the best deals, but nothing ever seems to fit. They don't like the mass obligation of Catholicism, the lack of central unity of the Baptist Church, the prohibition of alcohol and tobacco of Islam and the restrictions on sexual freedom of all religions. They search for something to call their own, but don't like the "whole' of any religion.

5B.   Informed Consumers know what they want and look into terms of ownership but only through renting, leasing, or exchanging. They get closer to God by seeking more information and personal assistance. They want to personalize and individualize the experience of God. People tend not to stay in this category because they wonder: should I buy? They know they'll never be satisfied unless their relationship with God belongs to them and they own it themselves.

5C.   Buyers take the first active step toward a relationship with God by wanting their own and actively seek to acquire it. They behave excitedly and work toward having a relationship to call their own.

6   Investors

6A.   Entrepreneurs do not pick and choose parts and pieces but desire an individual relationship with God through their own conscience. They see religion as a resource to obtain a closer personal relationship with God but seek a relationship with God, not a relationship with religion. They actively enter into a personal relationship with God because they believe that they have a personal calling, a special vocation for God.

6B. Franchisers want to work with others to deliver God to the world. They see how people working together can accomplish much more than individuals working separately or alone. They feel that they and others have something to offer and desire to bring people together, not for the benefit of the church, but for God.

7. Consumer Advocates seek a better product in the best interests of others. They want to connect people through religion and insure religion stays true to its responsibility to serve the community. They want to work in the best interest of all. They want religion to be responsible to every individual and to right the wrongs of society. While intolerance has been a historical part of every religion, Consumer Advocates point out where religion has served man instead of serving God. These people have taken their involvement from an intellectual level to an emotional level and from what they "think" to what they "feel." They work to assist in

bringing God into this world and feel man should serve God, not man.

8. Partners have a vested interest because they are owners, just as in the business world. They demonstrate increased personal involvement, responsibility and activity in their religious lives. They understand that their role is to work for the best interests of others; they know their eternal salvation is at stake, and they want to be actively involved in the process. They are aware of the societal and communal function of the church and while they want to help operate the institution of religion, they realize that they and God are partners in creating God's kingdom.

We move upward in this hierarchy of categories by becoming more personally involved with God through the realization that our journey is to God and not an institution. We may not be happy or satisfied with where we are, and if that is the case, we must move, but we are in the relationship we choose to be in.

CHAPTER TEN

Personal relationships

Jewish theologian Martin Buber wrote about types of relationships in I and thou.[17] According to Dr. Buber, the closest type of relationship is an *I-thou* relationship. Another person becomes a *thou* to us when we are aware of facts about the person and know them personally. *I-you* relationships define our relationships to others when that person is acknowledged as an individual but we don't know anything about them. Love at first sight happens when people fall in love with an idea of what the person is like (*I-you*), and only becomes love upon learning who that person really is as an individual (*I-thou*).

When people become objects to us they can become the enemy (them) or nonexistent (it). Problematic or even destructive relationships can result if we do not recognize others as individuals or if we do not know anything personal about them. *I-it* relationships happen when we fail to acknowledge others as people. While walking the dog, shopping, or being a spectator at a softball game, narcissists or self-absorbed individuals fail to recognize others as people, even reducing them to objects and attaching no value to them whatsoever. According to Dr. Buber, *I-it* relationships are the most dangerous type because *I-it* relationships can result in violence and evil.

I-it relationships disconnect us totally from others and isolate both parties. Then, disconnected, we strip identity and meaning from others and treat people as objects. We may assume that woman in the checkout line is being slow just to hold us up and not because she misplaced her credit card. When another car dangerously cuts in front of us, we may assume that the driver is cruel and uncaring. In reality, he may not have been aware that his lane ended and simply made a mistake. We're an object, an *it* to those people, and they're an *it* to us.

Test this theory yourself. Talk with relatives or acquaintances at gatherings and you may have a conversation that feels more like an interview. You may hear about someone's job, achievements, kids, and all the latest news in his life. After the conversation, ask yourself if the person knows anything about you that he didn't know before the conversation. If he doesn't, that's a telltale sign that he just used you as a sounding board to tell you about himself.

You were an *it*. He just spoke *at* you. We may find ourselves doing the same thing sometimes. We can constantly review our awareness and listening skills during conversations by asking ourselves if we know anything more about the other person after we're done talking. Listening and hearing is very different from giving out information. Being a good listener is a critical part of any relationship. Listening can help us clear up the mystery and the unknown in our relationship with God by helping us change our God from an *it* to a *thou* by familiarity.

At the wedding of one young couple, the priest spoke of how many people look at marriage as a 50-50 proposition, but it's not. It's a 100-100 proposition. We can't restrict relationships and expect to be satisfied with them. Both parties must invest totally in a relationship to make it work. In terms of doing the laundry or watching the kids if we say, "It's your turn" we make it sound as though marriage is a competition or contest. We may become preoccupied with keeping score and making sure everything stays even. If we enter any relationship worrying about keeping everything equal, we are preventing the relationship from flourishing and protecting ourselves from being taken advantage of.

It's natural to be attracted to people who are what we're not, who can complement us. As the old saying says, "Opposites attract," and it is sometimes true. A pioneer in nuclear research, Marie Curie, was a brilliant young Polish girl who married a widely acclaimed, absent-minded professor of Physics at The Sorbonne in Paris and who initially found the enthusiastic young girl annoying. Maybe we're attracted to someone outgoing or social because we're painfully shy, or we're drawn to an athlete because we're inactive and scholarly.

We might even use other people to satisfy our own needs or to make ourselves appear to be something we're not. Hollywood celebrity marriages that last for a few months seem to have nothing to do with love and everything to do with publicity and fame, or perhaps drinking too much, like Britney Spears 55 hour long marriage in January of 2004. By cheapening the institution of marriage, individuals minimize the commitment and vow, and treat it as meaningless.

When close romantic relationships with people go bad or don't work out, we feel devastated because our self-worth and security are damaged or even obliterated. We feel as if we are not desirable anymore. A woman might say, "We're just friends" about a former boyfriend who still longs to be more than just good friends. What she really means is, "He doesn't mean that much to me," which is a devastating message for the man.

Being friends is bad only in terms of unrequited love. In many ways close friends define our lives. We want people to want us. We want people to prefer us so we can feel desirable and better about ourselves. Many people dream about the cutest girl in class having a crush on them, or the captain of the football team paying them a lot of attention and making them feel popular and wanted like music and movie idols.

Popularity

People aspire to be held in high regard by others; we covet acknowledgement. We want attention, want to be most popular, want to win the trophy for chess club championship, to have our name in the newspaper, and to be named Most Valuable Player on our baseball team. Jesus himself would have been voted "most popular" on Palm Sunday when he was adored by the crowds and people placed palm branches down in front of him as he made a triumphant entrance into Jerusalem. But wait, those same people changed their minds and were partly responsible for putting Jesus to death on Good Friday.

That should provide us with a little perspective of how fickle public opinion is and how arbitrary fame and popularity are, but we still chase after both. It matters to us what people think of us. Our self-image and self-acceptance are tied to the acceptance of others. Our insecurity puts us at the mercy of other people's judgments and expectations to such an extent that it becomes very important for us to fit in socially. Think back to the most popular guys and girls in grade school or high school, then fast-forward twenty years. Those same people probably are not the most popular now. They are no longer the object of everyone else's envy, as they were long ago.

Imagine seeing an old classmate who is now a millionaire or winner of a prestigious award. "I didn't know," we might say. "If I'd have known he would be so rich and famous, I would have treated him better and I would have been nicer to him." Consider how we would treat him and how that would change his credibility. According to Jesus' ideal of how we should treat people, the overweight, quirky introvert we work with who seems to be a social misfit should get the same concern from us as the Chief Executive

Officer of a Fortune 500 Company, the sports hero or the music star. The point of God's message is that we should be treating everyone the same regardless of their achievements, accomplishments or placement in life.

Growing up, holding hands for the first time or getting a first kiss can consume our thoughts. We must be okay if someone else wants to hold our hand, touch us and actually kiss us! Romantic relationships have an amazing power over our self-esteem and it's easy to cling to them too tightly: that's our self-acceptance we're holding onto. The popular high school couple that suddenly breaks up might plunge either or both parties into a depression and melancholy when the relationship ends.

As we stumble through awkward and embarrassing relationships, it's natural to appeal to God and whine, "Why are all my relationships turning out so bad? Why does this have to happen to me, I'm a nice person!?" It's easy to blame God for not giving us a good romantic relationship, but if we take the time to be honest we'll admit that, even if we're lucky, all our romantic relationships fail except one. The only time we won't get hurt is if we end up getting married and staying happily married to someone we love. Relationships have to do with us and all the focus is on our personal needs.

The best thing we can do for our relationships is to accept ourselves as we are, not use other people to make us what we're not. Such a person is not needy, nor does she depend on someone else to complete her personality. A relationship will not fill in missing pieces but add to what is already there. We can enter a relationship with everything to offer and be the kind of person someone else would want to be around if we don't require that person to fix our problems or make us what we ourselves are not.

Kalil Gibran spoke of relationships in *The Prophet*. "Stand together yet not too near together: For the pillars of the temple stand apart, and the oak tree and the cypress grow not in each others' shadow."[18] In our relationships we are like those trees. If they are planted too close, neither one will grow completely full. If we expect any person or institution other than God to complete us we will always be incomplete.

We can expand and grow when we allow our relationship with God and others to add to us. Al Cecchi, the CEO of Northwest Orient Airlines, dedicated a high school addition in memory of classmate and teammate Bobby Rafferty and said, "It's not what you are born with, but what you do with it. It's not how much you take, but what you give. It's not about the quantities that you attain, but the quality. And what ultimately defines a man is his relationships, with God and his fellow man."

Healthy relationships are not always fair but they are mutual. Frequently someone in a relationship is going to get hurt, and it's not always anyone's fault. Sometimes one person is much more interested and involved with the relationship than the other and this kind of mismatch often cannot be easily predicted or avoided.

When Vince Lombardi was coach of the Green Bay Packers football team in the 1960's, someone mentioned that Paul Horning, a player who had a reputation as a notorious womanizer, was going out with a large number of women. Lombardi very seriously asked, "Can't he find one he likes?" Forming meaningful relationships is not a popularity contest or a numbers game, but we like the idea of being popular and having everyone desire us.

Being told someone likes us if flattering. Our ego loves it. Usually when we find out someone likes us, we think, "That's nice, but I really don't like her that much, and I really wish someone like Beyonce liked me." We want people to like us but we want to decide who we like. All we are really searching for, however, is a person to love and love us back, but we want the option of changing our mind in case we love someone else. Being connected in a relationship begins with us taking a chance to allow other people to see us figuratively naked.

Hiding

When I was growing up I tried to pretend that I could hide from God. Whenever I was embarrassed about something I had done or something I didn't like about myself, I would pretend that if I didn't admit to it, it didn't exist or never really happened. No one knew I cheated on my Spanish quiz or about the candy I stole from the Seven Eleven. I could deny cheating and taking the candy and I wanted to believe I could fool God, too.

Looking back, I guess I wanted my relationship to be like today's chat rooms on the Internet, where

God wouldn't know anything about me except what I volunteered and I could withhold information or make things up without God being any the wiser. I would do this to create an improved but false image of myself so God would like me because I didn't want to be exposed and I wasn't so sure I was likeable.

I tried to keep my relationship with God compartmentalized, separate and apart from my life. I did not want God to see all of me, and that prevented me from forming a close, honest relationship with God. I felt guilty knowing I was lying to God, but being insecure and afraid of rejection, I was afraid of what God would think of me if God knew the "real me" and that God wouldn't like me. Taking responsibility for every facet of my character would leave me totally naked in front of God, both physically and mentally, and that was a situation I wanted to avoid. I didn't want to consider that God could get inside my head and see everything that was there and see how imperfect I was.

The 1977 movie *Oh, God!* was about a normal, average guy played by John Denver and George Burns played the part of God. In one scene, John Denver was taking a shower when he heard God's voice. As John hurriedly tried to cover himself, God said, "I'm God, I know what you've got." Those words reminded me that it was a waste of time trying to hide things from God. God knows everything about us, even what we deny about ourselves, and God even knows why we try to hide those things.

We can deceive, cheat, and lie, but God is aware of our every act and thought. God knows that the omission of income on our tax return was no mistake, God knows about our marital indiscretion that no one else knows. We may be able to fool other people and let them see what we want them to see. We may even be able to fool ourselves, but we must honestly admit that God sees everything.

Knowing that God sees everything about us might help us honestly face exactly who we are. No matter how often we pretend that we don't need God's assistance, God is always with us ready and willing to help us to help us face who we really are and honestly accept ourselves. God is aware of all the imperfections that make us human, knows everything both good and bad about us and loves us anyway without conditions or reservations.

When God gave a mission to the prophet Jonah to go and warn the enemies of the Israelites to change their ways or face wrath, Jonah resisted God and attempted to flee in a boat because the last thing he wanted to do was work to save his enemies. He was swallowed by a whale and remained there for three days until he had a change of heart. When Jonah admitted he was wrong, accepted God's will and stopped trying to run from God, he was "spit out" from the belly of the whale.

Unlike our relationships with people, our relationship with God is permanent and honest and God is always with us. Nothing is more important to God than we are. God not only likes us but loves us, even though we are so insecure we might ask, "Are you sure?" Instead of worrying about keeping our relationship with God, we should be thinking about how to get closer to God.

We do not seek a relationship with God, we already have a relationship with God. What we determine is what type of relationship we will have. We decide how close we are to God. To understand our connection with God we must first attempt to find where we are in relation to God. We are in fact associated, related, and involved with God through Jesus Christ's blood.

We and God are family. God has already made clear the desire to be as close to us as possible by sending Jesus to earth. Jesus explained that there is a bond between us and God, saying that we are heirs to the kingdom of Heaven. We are the ones who will decide how we respond to God.

Many times we complain how everyone is out to get us, using the "poor, poor, pitiful, me" routine as if we are always the victim; but maybe we have to keep a mirror handy so we can take a look at ourselves and see if our stubbornness, inflexibility, fear of commitment, or desire to be in control are the causes of our relationship problems. We may also cause the problems in our relationship with God. God loves us perfectly so if we aren't close to God, God hasn't moved away from us, we have moved away from God.

As long as we believe in God as a vindictive headmaster, we will fear and try to avoid God. If we are afraid of God and our relationship with God, our lives will be spent fearing God's punishment. But the Christian God wants what's best for us and punishment is always a last resort. God represents the good that is possible for us and our world. Albert Einstein once stated, "Either nothing is a miracle or everything is a miracle." When asked if he believed in miracles, Buddha replied that every change of heart is a miracle. The real miracle is God's love for us.

CHAPTER ELEVEN

Putting God in our life

The desire to know about God and expecting to find all the answers is like randomly opening a book and expecting to know what the book is about by reading a few words, or opening the Bible and trying to find a meaningful, inspirational quote. We can't achieve either goal without effort and we can't do it piecemeal. To find our answers, we have to read the whole book. Trying to run a marathon without training will not yield great results; neither will expecting to get God into our life without making room for God.

We are constantly bombarded with ads and info-mercials in the media selling ways to make everything easier. Nutrition, weight-loss, body-building, health and fitness, even house-cleaning products promise great results with a minimum of effort. We want those "six-pack" abdominal muscles we see on some people and even do a hundred sit-ups a day to strengthen our muscles, but if we have thirty pounds of fat covering our stomach we might not see any difference at all in our waistline.

When we drive, we want to know how far over the speed limit we can go and still not get a ticket. Similarly, we wonder if we really need to go to mass and if we have to go to mass every week. Once we're at mass we may wonder how long we must stay to get credit for attending. If we are seduced by the idea of getting something for nothing we might want our relationship with God to be easy too. It's as if we're asking God for a participation credit just by showing up. We want the secret potion that will instantly heal our spiritual wounds, ease our doubts and provide us with the answers to all our questions about God, but it doesn't exist.

We can develop an attitude wondering, "How much do I have to do?" to bring God into our life by taking short cuts, seeking a pacifier rather than a solution. Instead of wondering how we can take the easy way out, we might want to think about how people master a skill, like being a professional athlete or musician. It's unfair for us to expect to be exceptional at singing, running, or surgery without practice.

Preparation provides a way to achieve a goal, whether it's losing weight, getting more skilled at playing a musical instrument or being more competent at balancing our checkbook, we know what we have to do and decide whether its worth the effort or not. We won't get closer to God by going through the drive-through window at our convenience but by placing ourselves at God's disposal and putting forth our best effort.

A diet may work for a few weeks or months, but if we go back to overeating we will end up regaining any weight we lost. A temporary fix will not work, but a permanent lifestyle change, such as reducing fat and eliminating chocolates and sugar from our diet, will help us reach our desired result. We can't approach God and our spiritual health like a "yo-yo" diet where we periodically make some effort to bring God into our life and expect to be satisfied.

Our bodies have a very short memory. They respond amazingly well to work. If we won an event at the Olympics, we would have attained an elite level of performance after many years of work and sacrifice. If we stopped exercising over the next few months, our bodies would return to the same shape as people who never did any physical activity. We need to practice hard for a long period of time to perform at an exceptionally high level, and we also need to keep practicing to maintain that level.

We can't pay attention to our relationship with God only when we need something, nor should we treat God like a vending machine or like a salesman who shows up at our door. Ignoring him does not mean he isn't there; it simply means we choose not to respond to him. Our relationship with God should be a constant priority and we should work at it with determination and dedication. The hard part, like with a diet, is having the discipline to make God the main focus in our lives.

We need to think about God and make God a larger part of our daily lives. We might find it hard to get God into all the little compartments of our lives at work, at school and during our leisure time, but that's our challenge. We need to practice God more. Everything we do reflects our relationship with God. Not just participating in Sunday services and putting a "I love Jesus" bumper sticker on our car or door, but how we respond to every action.

As we struggle with the question of how to follow God, simply being aware of God can help us stay focused on our spiritual life and become concerned, not with how much we have to do, but how much more we can do. Christians should be acting as Jesus would every second of every day, thinking about how God is a part of our lives every moment.

Writers Cynthia Sterling and Megan Davidson tell this story to illustrate our   expectations of developing a relationship with God.

"One day while waiting to board an airplane, a writer struck up a conversation with a pleasant gentleman. The man revealed that he was a surgeon. 'And you?' he asked the writer.

'I write novels,' she replied.

'That's interesting,' said the doctor. 'You know, someday I'd like to write a novel, too.'

The writer nodded. 'Yes, she sighed. I know what you mean. Someday I'd like to perform a coronary bypass.'[19]

The doctor assumed that writing a novel took no preparation, no special effort, and would simply happen, and we may act the same way about our relationship with God. To desire a relationship with God and assume it just happens as if by magic or by joining a religion is like trying to write a novel without learning the craft of writing, or performing heart surgery without extensive training.

Where do we put God?

We must be aware of the investment of effort and personal involvement we must make to get closer to God. In our relationship with God, the pressure to change is on us, not God, but we have to change from within and do it completely. Visiting God at church is easy because keeping God away from our daily life keeps religion in its place and our "real" lives in another. Wanting to get God into our life while not working to bring God into every moment can lead us to make a special compartment to put God in, a doghouse or guest-quarters to keep God away from us and separate from where we live.

If we decide to open the door and answer God's knock, how do we answer? We might meet God at church like we would the pizza delivery guy, on the front porch where we can access God when we choose but keep God outside. We might be so cluttered up inside there's no room for God, or we might want to hide parts of ourselves from God.

We might be shopping for God as we would at an antique shop (God is really old) or at a flea market hoping to find a trophy. We might be browsing for God without having any place to put God in our lives. If God were a beautiful old chest of drawers we found at a yard sale would we say, "Now where am I going to put this?"

God is not an adornment but the central piece we build our lives around. We can attend mass regularly, serve on committees and boards, volunteer and belong to service organizations, but if we aren't doing these activities to get closer to God, then we are simply fulfilling a perceived obligation to a church. We may keep God separate from our "real" life by always going away to visit God, but when can God come over to our house?

Even if it is easier for us to keep God away from where we live and who we really are, God awaits the invitation to come into our life. When it comes to furnishing our lives we are all packrats. Our days are cluttered with our own concerns, wants, and desires, and God can enter our lives when and if we clear some room to put God in. We must get rid of some of our clutter if we are to let God in. Like a cup filled to the top with water, if we are full of our own ideas and opinions, there is no room for God.

My friend Terri once listed all her decisions and concerns for one day and separated them into two groups. One group listed her concerns for staying alive for that day; the other listed her concerns for trying to improve the comfort of her life. One list itemized what she needed and the other what she wanted. She was surprised to discover that she hardly paid any attention at all to the food, clothing, shelter, and warmth needed for her survival; instead she was preoccupied with things to make her life more comfortable, like buying a new car, getting a promotion at work and upgrading her cell phone.

If our relationship with God is a fundamental concern for us, we should consider allowing God to be a part of every decision we make and allow God to become a need as well as a desire. We often ask for help making a decision when all we really want is validation. God isn't here just to say, "Yes" to us, but God *is here*. We aren't alone. In every decision we make, God is right with us, and we have the option of getting God's help whenever we want it.

If we suppress some of our selfish desires, God can dwell in us. In a letter to her sister, Sister Theresa of Lysieux wrote in *Collected Letters:* "If you are willing to serenely bear the trial of being displeasing to yourself, then you will be for Jesus a pleasant place of shelter."[20] If we want to strip a piece of wooden furniture, we take off any damaged portions before staining the piece. If we want to improve our lives, we have to make room for God. We can't just keep covering up our problems like putting new wallpaper over old. The search for God cannot be from religious obligation from the outside-in; the search for God must be a personal desire from the inside-out. Finding God is not a mystery; it's a choice. It can't be a half-hearted attempt but our absolute best effort by being competitive.

Being Competitive

With our trophy mentality, we want to compete. To compete involves a contest for a prize or honor.

Our salvation and heaven are prizes that await us, so why aren't we more concerned with obtaining them? Being called "competitive" gets an immediate positive or negative response from people who are either proud or defensive. Some people believe being competitive means winning at all costs, like succeeding in the business world.

Many of us don't want to be seen as overly competitive or obsessed with winning, but at the same time we all want to win and we are all at least somewhat competitive. Our level of competitiveness determines how far we will go to win and sometimes can lead us to compromise our integrity, cheat, or lie to gain an unfair advantage and improve our chances of winning.

Saying we aren't competitive tends to infer that not being competitive is a virtue. We want everyone to be treated equally, so we give trophies to every member of our kindergarten T-ball team. "Participation trophies" result when involvement, not the outcome, is our only concern. Participation awards are the communism of involvement; they are independent of our individual effort because we're getting our reward regardless of how we perform. These awards might have great significance to us as a six-year-old, but they may rightfully become meaningless to us as we grow older.

Those who want to dictate the outcome, to have everyone finish equally, with no winners or losers, are in reality closet competitors or passive competitors, dictating the results of the competition and removing the pressure to perform by assuring that the result is the same regardless of the effort. When we remove any involvement on our part, we remove any personal responsibility for our performance. If every worker on the job gets the same amount of money, there is no incentive to try and work harder.

At one time, being competitive was considered a good thing. It meant trying as hard as possible and doing the absolute best we could, placing all the responsibility for winning on our performance and effort. Losing meant either accepting defeat, giving up and quitting, or working hard to improve. Everyone wants to win while they're playing the game, but we may not be willing to put in the days, weeks, and months of necessary preparation leading up to the game. Similarly, we all want to go to heaven and obtain salvation, but do we care enough to prepare ourselves for heaven today? Our relationship with God depends on our performance and effort every day.

To be competitive is to put more effort into preparation as well as into the game. The point of competitiveness is our effort, especially in our preparation for heaven. Would we rather play well and lose, or play poorly and win? Would we rather play all the time on a lousy team or never play on a championship team?

At Argyle Country Club in Silver Spring, Maryland, there was only one Junior (under 18) girl who played golf, so the club decided to place the girl into the boy's bracket of the junior championship. When they heard about this, the girl's parents asked whether she was still going to receive the trophy for being the girl's champion.

Competition is preparation and effort; a measure of how much we want to challenge ourselves. Our lives will be over before we know it, and our measure of success will come from how satisfied we feel about our performance. As students finish their final exams to complete college, they think back on the whole experience at school. Their feelings of satisfaction should depend on how hard they worked. Hopefully, the harder they worked, the more satisfied they feel and the fewer regrets they have. The satisfaction we feel in our life is our success.

Compared to God

Luke 18:10 – 14 says: *Two people went up to the temple area to pray; one was a Pharisee and the other was a tax collector. The Pharisee took up his position and spoke this prayer to himself, 'O God, thank you that I am not like the rest of humanity -greedy, dishonest, adulterous-or even like this tax-collector. I fast twice a week, and I pay tithes on my whole income.' But the tax collector stood off at a distance and would not even raise his eyes to heaven but beat his breast and prayed, 'O God be merciful to me a sinner.' I tell you, the latter went home justified, not the former for everyone who exalts himself will be humbled, and everyone who humbles himself will be exalted.*

The Pharisee was comparing himself to humans. The tax collector was comparing himself to God and that's why he was so humble. Compared to God we're not very impressive. The tax collector, a Jew who took money from his countrymen and gave it to the occupying Romans, was one of the most despised individuals in Jesus' time, but because he kept his sight on God he pleased God. For Jesus to show the tax collector in a favorable light was shocking to his audience.

Like the tax collector, the only person we should be competing *with* is ourselves, and the only person we should be comparing ourselves *to* is God. Competition provides us with a measure of our performance. Remembering our trophy case mentality can help us remember what we hope to accomplish as we assemble the pieces to build our lives and compare ourselves to everyone else by our credentials, house, car, job, money, and associations. Using our possessions to measure our worth is the opposite of Jesus' message.

We can recall what is important from God's point of view and focus on accomplishments from Jesus' perspective: how well we model Jesus' teachings. Jesus preached that what is important is not just participating but giving our best effort to create God's kingdom.

Although we might wonder how this applies to us today as we sit in a church or among neighbors; we constantly compare ourselves to those around us. We can pick apart and find fault with anyone. We might say and think that he drinks too much, point out that she has been married a few times, say that those parents are verbally abusive toward or neglect their children. When we compare ourselves to each other, we presume a lot about people, just like little kids making fun of each other saying you're fat, ugly, or stupid, and we need to remember that we're all imperfect and compare ourselves to God.

God challenges us to be the best mother, father, sister, brother, friend, neighbor, employer, employee, husband, coach, or student we can be. Jesus promised the Holy Spirit to provide us with the strength to help us. The success of our lives, the trophies that matter, will be the instances of "agape," the Greek word for unconditional love we have shown. Our success will be measured through the satisfaction of knowing we gave our best effort trying to build God's kingdom. We must perform, and as St. Bernadette said, "I must become a Saint, my Jesus expects it."

Being competitive is at the core of what Jesus lived and preached. Laura Hillenbrand wrote *Seabiscuit: An American Legend,* a bestselling book in 2001 that became a hit movie. It tells the story of an undersized, crooked-legged horse named Seabiscuit, who defied all odds and won races during the American depression. When people needed a hero, the horse exhibited a competitiveness rarely seen by any animal.

Very few people have this depth of competitive spirit. When we do hear a story of strength and overcoming hardship we should be inspired. We should also be challenged to do the same. Competition is a positive word. Being competitive is striving for the best, not compromising, and not holding back anything from our effort in our relationships or endeavors. By seeing God as our strength we can get over our feelings of inadequacy or lack of ability and embrace the challenge of doing God's work. Even if we think we're not worthy, God has work that needs to be done. Christianity is the call to ultimate competitiveness and competition, the call to put all of our effort and preparation into working for God through each other. To maintain a clear focus of what God wants from us, we must stay in constant contact with God. Just as we do with friends, we must stay in touch.

CHAPTER TWELVE

Contact with God

Jesus taught that we could all personally have unmediated, direct contact with God. We can speak with God through prayer. Prayer comes from the Latin *precarious:* granted as a favor or obtained by begging, and *precari:* to entreat, ask earnestly, beseech, or implore. A petition is a prayer for oneself, while an intercession is on behalf of another, but both are communication with God done without the assistance of an operator. Reciting the Hail Mary, Rosary or special memorized prayers from a book may help us contact God, but they're not the only prayers that are heard, because God always hears us.

There are many different positions from which to pray. Muslims kneel and bow in prayer always facing east, in the direction of the holy city, Mecca. Catholics kneel to pray. Jews recite prayers while "davaning", or bowing repeatedly. Buddhists assume the lotus position taught in yoga by bending the legs and crossing the ankles while placing their arms with palm's facing up in their lap to meditate. For Buddhists, this position is reminiscent of the position that the Buddha once assumed while fighting evil. A Hindu is taught to sit facing east and sprinkle water around himself and the god-image being meditated on. Prayer beads are used as well as offerings of flowers, scents, incense, candles, and special food for the god.

What are we to make of this variety of prayer and positions? If praying the Our Father leads us to focus on God, then it is serving its purpose. If reciting memorized words or kneeling distracts us from what we want to communicate with God about, then we should stop praying in that way, but we should continue praying. Kneeling, bowing, or bending our legs to pray may distract us. The intent of certain words or certain positions is to focus our minds on praying, but we can't allow any routine to distract us from the purpose of communicating with God.

In Matthew 6:7-8 we are told not just to say words and be concerned with the routine, ritual, or form we follow but to speak earnestly because God knows what is in our heart as well as what is on our lips. "In praying, do not babble like the pagans who think that they will be heard because of their many words. Do not be like them. Your Father knows what you need before you ask him." Our attitude and intent are more important than the words we use, our physical position, or whether the prayer is spoken out loud or thought. Prayer is simply an attitude of being aware of and receptive to God.

It seems curious that at the moment we attempt to contact the highest power in the universe we usually seem to do all the talking rather than listening. If we saw a friend on the street and began reading from a pamphlet instead of starting a conversation with them, it would be as if our friend were not in front of us at all. Praying through rote memorization without being aware that we are speaking to God is just like reading from a pamphlet in God's presence, being lost in the form of how we pray rather than being aware of the function of communicating with God.

So how are we supposed to pray, and what are we supposed to say to make sure God hears us? The answer depends on the faith of the person you ask.

When at a seminar on prayer, one of the participants asked the presenter, "Doctor, how should I pray?"

"It's very simple," the noted expert responded without hesitation "Ask God."[21]

A little girl asked her teacher, who was a nun, what the best prayer was and the nun responded, "Say, my life is my prayer."

Books on prayer are big business, and there have been many best-selling books about praying. *The Prayer of Jabez* by Bruce Wilkinson was a best-selling book which claimed that God enjoys saying yes to prayers and giving us what we wish for. The book is based on an obscure Old Testament story about a man who recited a certain prayer every day and ultimately got riches beyond his belief. The premise of the book is that if we say and believe as Jabez did, we too will get great riches from God, and when we get more we can do more for God.

Our trophy-case mentality of wanting a reward appears even when we communicate with God. This sounds as if we're playing "Let's make a deal" with God and assumes that we can do more for God if we're wealthy. Another book by Mr. Wilkinson: *A Life God Rewards,* strongly suggests by it's title that our performance will result in some sort of reward from God, a trophy for our effort.

This is consistent with the perception that God should give us things. People with this sort of mentality expect to receive something for performing a task, like a dog that has performed a trick. Sayings we hear every day refer to our being a winner or a loser. Having a "trophy wife," hearing, "You're golden," being in "a win-win situation," getting "your just reward," and being "a deserving person," or "close, but no cigar" all have to do with obtaining something. Even in our communication with God we are programmed to win. We don't always want what's in our spiritual best interests; we want to *get* something.

Some people may think of prayer in a very mercenary way. Prayer can be thought of as being made in to a genie in a lamp where we have to rub the lamp the right way or say just the right words in order to elicit a response. Prayer can be made to a game show host who might respond, "I'm sorry, you didn't phrase that in the form of a question" or "Those are not the correct words, so your request is denied." Prayer can even be made to a slot machine that allows us to hit the big jackpot every once in a while. The opposite of praying to receive something is praying to express gratefulness and thanks for the gifts we already have.

Our prayers should be a celebration of the fact that God chose to save us. Jesus brought us forgiveness for our failings and imperfections, grace, and salvation. We have those things now and they are our riches. Prayer is not a wish list, like children write to Santa. Prayer is our way of extending an open hand to God without expectations. Prayer is a way for us to say *please* and *thank you* to God.

Prayer is our attempt to contact God to make sure that we are headed in the right direction, simply listening to know what's next, or to concede that we need help with a task that we can't handle by ourselves. William McGill wrote, "The value of consistent prayer is not that he hear us, but that we hear him." Just as we call our friends and family to check on them and see how they are, we can check in with God through prayer. Prayer is supplication; that's why so many people kneel in prayer, since kneeling is the position we take when pleading our case. Mahatma Gandhi wrote, "Prayer is a confession of one's own unworthiness and weakness."

James Mulholland, a minister in Indianapolis who wrote *Praying like Jesus,* states, "The whole point of prayer is not to tell God what you want, but to hear what you need." Mike Nappa, in *The Prayer of Jesus*, writes, "The Lord's Prayer is not a formula to guarantee that God will always bless you but a model for pursuing intimacy with God."

In the early 1990's a doctor named Larry Dossey compiled all the experimental information he could on prayer and physical healing. He found that many scientific experiments had been done using prayer with over half of them "Showing scientifically significant changes in a variety of living beings" from humans to bacterial cultures.

Many experiments showed that prayer works and non-directed prayer, which specifies no particular outcome, works even better than praying for a specific outcome. Prayer was shown to be effective in helping individuals improve their condition, even when the people being prayed for were unaware anyone was praying for them. In his book *Healing Words,* Doctor Dossey came to the point that he reasoned not to employ prayer with his patients would be equivalent to deliberately withholding a potent drug or surgical procedure from them.

Prayer works wonders when individuals pray with the attitude of leaving all decisions up to God, as in, "Thy will be done." Prayer is not telling God what to do. Cited in Dr. Dossey's book, Aldous Huxley proposed a Law of Reversed Effort, which theorizes that, "The more we try to push and control these events, the more the desired result seems to elude us. The secret seems to consist in not trying and not doing, allowing the world to manifest its wisdom, not ours."[22] "Let go and let God" is one way of saying that the intent of prayer is for us to contact God for directions, and allow God to act.

Doctor Dossey mentioned that when we *try* to have fun we usually fail. When we try to tell God what to do, our attempts will probably fail. Prayer seems to elicit the best response when directed at whatever is in the best interests of the organism (whether the organism is a bacterium or a human). This advice provides little consolation to someone who has lost a family member or friend to illness despite constant prayer, but it should offer the possibility that God has done what was best for the organism. Doctor Dossey states, "Prayer works 100% of the time, unless we prevent this realization by remaining oblivious to it."[23] Francis Cardinal Spellman put it this way: "Pray as if everything depends on God, act as if everything depends on you."

One episode of the television show M*A*S*H, a 1970's comedy set at a front line surgical hospital during the Korean War, was about a bomber pilot who thought he was Christ. When the camp Chaplain, Father Mulkahey, asked the pilot, "Is it true God answers all our prayers?" the pilot answered, "Yes."

"Then why don't we get everything we ask for?" Father asked.

The pilot replied, "Sometimes the answer is no."

This comment echoes the sentiment of a church signboard that read: "God gives three answers: yes, no, and wait."

We must admit there are things we don't know and can't explain. Buddhist teachings that summarize effective prayer advise us to: "Have good intent." There seems to be no correct way to pray. To pray, it seems, is correct. Prayer is an attitude. Maybe a better description of what could help us keep the lines of communication open between ourselves and God is called "prayerfulness," which implies respect and humility,

Prayer itself is indefinable. One small study done in September 1951 was the Prayer Experiment at the University of Redlands in Redlands California, which was popularized in a book *Prayer Can Change Your Life* by Dr. William R. Parker and Elaine St. Johns.[24] This experiment, which seemed to scientifically have many flaws, involved three groups of individuals. Group I did not mention prayer at all, Group II included Christians who did not request any assistance in their prayers, and Group III offered guidance and assistance to individuals in their prayers.

At the end of the experiment, only Group II showed no improvement in their physical health. How could people who prayed be less effective than those who didn't pray at all? Maybe the result goes back to the intent of the individuals. Could the Group II individuals have adopted an attitude that somehow left out the need for assistance? Prayer *is* a request for help and assistance, so maybe when we assume we can do it all by ourselves, it isn't prayer at all; maybe then we're just telling God what to do or what we want.

A dying man was asked by Dr. Dossey, "What do you pray for?"

"I don't pray for anything," He responded.

"How would I know what to ask for?"

This was surprising. Surely this dying man could think of *some* request.

"If prayer is not for asking, what is it *for*?"

'It isn't 'for' anything," he said thoughtfully. It mainly reminds me I am not alone."[25]

Regarding the studies on prayer, Dr. Dossey observed, "No longer will we pray for *things*, such as our health, but our prayers will be predominantly prayers of gratitude and thanksgiving-our proper response on realizing that the world, at heart, is more glorious, benevolent, and friendlier than we have recently supposed."[26]

Doctor Dossey himself had a spiritual advisor who told him to try to pray at certain set times during the day. When he asked why, he was told that he should not only pray to God when it was convenient for him, but he should also communicate with God when it was convenient for God.[27] Calling a friend on the phone and only talking when we feel like it, but expecting her to stay on the line indefinitely is unrealistic, and so is our expectation for God to be our personal attendant. The spiritual advisor was reminding the Doctor to remember that he should be the one accommodating God, it was he who was trying to contact God and enlist God's assistance.

68 year old Franciscan friar Mychal F. Judge, a New York City Fire Department chaplain, was killed in the World Trade Center bombing of 9/11. In his pocket he carried a prayer he had written himself: "Lord, take me where You want me to go; Let me meet who You want me to meet; tell me what You want me to say, and keep me out of Your way." This prayer illustrates an attitude of acceptance and request for guidance that our prayers should place in God's hands. One gentleman even ended his prayers by saying, "Lord make me invisible so that they see me less and you more." Through our prayers we should

be putting ourselves at God's disposal by saying, just as Jesus did as he cried out while hanging from the cross, "Into your hands I place my spirit."

Persistence

Jesus himself speaks to his disciples in the gospel of Luke (11:9 - 13) saying,

> *"Suppose you went to a friend's house at midnight, wanting to borrow three loaves of bread. You would shout up to him, 'A friend of mine has just arrived for a visit and I've nothing to give him to eat.' He would call down from his bedroom, 'Please don't ask me to get up. The door is locked for the night and we are all in bed. I just can't help you this time.' 'But I'll tell you this-though he won't do it as a friend, if you keep knocking long enough, he will get up and get you everything you want-just because of your persistence. And so it is with prayer-ask and you will receive; look and you will find; knock and the door will be opened.*
>
> *Everyone who asks, receives; all who seek, find; and the door is opened to everyone who knocks. You men who are fathers-if your boy asks you for bread, do you give him a stone? If he asks for fish, do you give him a snake? If he asks for an egg, do you give him a scorpion? And even if sinful persons like yourselves give children what they need,*

*don't you realize your Heavenly Father will
do at least as much, and give the Holy Spirit
to those who ask for him? Do for others what
you would have them do for you."*

We may not get what we want or an immediate
response because sometimes God says, "Wait" but if
we are persistent, God will respond with what is best
for us. Jesus is asking for our trust in this passage.
He is telling all of us that every request, every single
effort on our part will be answered by God if we
have faith.

CHAPTER THIRTEEN

Faith and Action

Our faith in God and belief in the Lord's direction is our treasure and wealth, the substance upon which our lives are built. Our faith, then, not any acquisition, is a trophy. Matthew 6:19 - 21 says:

> *Do not store up for yourselves treasures on earth, where moth and decay destroy, and thieves break in and steal. For where your treasure is, there also will your heart be. Therefore I tell you, do not worry about your life, what you will eat or drink or about your body, what you will wear. Is not life more than food and the body more than clothing? Look at the birds in the sky; they do not sow or reap, they gather nothing into barns, yet your heavenly Father feeds them. Are you not more important than they? Can any of you add a single moment to your life by worrying?*

Why are you anxious about clothes? Learn from the way the wild flowers grow. They do not work or spin. But I tell you not even Solomon in all his splendor was clothed like one of them. If God so clothes the grass of the field, which grows today and is thrown into the oven tomorrow, will he not much more provide for you, O you of little faith? So do not worry and say, 'What are we to eat?' or 'What are we to drink?' or 'What are we to wear?' Your Heavenly Father knows what you need. Seek first the kingdom of God and his righteousness, and all these things will be given to you. Do not worry about tomorrow, it will take care of itself. Today brings enough worries.

This passage reminds us that the meaning and accomplishments we seek are found by seeking God and God's kingdom. Jesus sent his disciples out after his resurrection with no money, food, or extra clothes. The only direction or agenda he gave them was to go out and spread the good news. He told them he would give them everything they needed if they had faith in him. That doesn't mean he was suggesting that they passively leave everything up to God; it meant that God would provide absolutely everything they needed if they trusted in God. Jesus tells us we should allow God to guide us and that God will take care of the rest. As we surround ourselves with our daily worries, we should remember what Jesus told Martha in the gospel of Luke 10:38 - 42:

As Jesus and his disciples went on their way, he came to a certain village where a woman named Martha welcomed him in her home. She had a sister named Mary, who sat down at the feet of the Lord, and listened to his teaching. Martha was upset over all of the work that she had to do; so she came and said, "Lord, don't you care that my sister has left me to do all the work by myself? Tell her to come and help me!"

The Lord answered her, "Martha, Martha! You are worried and troubled over so many things, but just one is needed. Mary has chosen the right thing, and it will not be taken from her."

We make decisions regarding the direction of our lives. We may not be able to see the map, but we can understand where we want to go. We must persevere and trust that God will do what is best for us and give us our directions. Jesus told Martha only one thing is required: to seek God. All of our other concerns and worries can be dealt with by listening to Jesus' message. We must have faith in God. Luke 17:5 - 6 tells us:

And the apostles said to the Lord, "Increase our faith." The Lord replied, "If you have faith the size of a mustard seed, you would say to this Mulberry tree, 'Be uprooted in the sea,' and it would obey you."

We may never know God's timetable or direction, but we are directed to pray without ceasing and have faith in God. We need no better example of how we are being asked to trust God than that of Jesus' mother Mary. For a young girl two thousand years ago, adultery and becoming pregnant outside of marriage meant the end of a normal life for a woman.

Angels told Mary that she was pregnant when she was unmarried and very young. She responded by submitting to God's plan for her, even though she didn't understand what that plan was. She trusted that God was acting in her best interest, accepted the Angels message and left the rest to God. She let go and let (allowed) God. If Mary wasn't sure, how can we expect to be sure what God's plan is for us? Our faith is, like Mary's, acknowledgement and trust in God.

Jesus himself agonized over his role in God's plan in the garden before his Passion. He reached the point, as we should, where he surrendered to God and said, "Not my will, but yours be done." Throughout the gospels Jesus cures people and tells them their faith has been their salvation. Jesus taught that faith is the difference between what happens and what doesn't happen. Having faith in God is the anchor that stabilizes our lives.

A small girl who was visiting her grandparents went out on a little boat with her Grandpa to learn how to fish. When they reached the spot on the lake where her Grandpa wanted to fish from, he handed the girl the rope and told her to throw the anchor overboard. Being eight years old and never having been on a boat before, the little girl followed directions in the literal way children often do and threw the rope *and* the anchor overboard. The girl's grandpa realized that it wasn't her fault, because he had failed to tell her exactly what to do. He told her that whenever she threw out an anchor, she had to make sure that she first fastened the rope securely to the boat.

If we let go and have faith enough to allow God to work in our lives, we must first make sure that we are securely anchored to God. If we don't, we're just throwing our faith overboard. Similarly, like a branch of a tree, we cannot survive if we are detached from our base. God is our base and we must remain attached to God to produce fruit through our actions.

After Jesus told the disciples the manner in which he would die, Peter told Jesus not to allow it. In Mark 8:27 - 32 Jesus told Peter, "Get behind me, Satan." Some theologians believe he was telling Peter to stop doubting God, stop pretending to know what's best, and trust in God. Other scholars claim Jesus meant, "Don't stand in my way, don't tempt me." In either case, Jesus was reminding Peter to listen to and accept; to let go and support Gods direction.

Faith is what we need to allow God to use us in the manner God wants. If we are players on God's team, sometimes we might end up playing a position we don't want to play. We might even end up doing something we don't want to, like Simon the Cyrenian who was called upon to carry Christ's cross as Jesus was led to his crucifixion. We must trust God enough to allow ourselves to be used by God for the good of the team.

Jesus himself knew how our faith is revealed through our actions. Mark 2:1 - 12 says:

When Jesus returned to Capernaum after some days, it became known that he was at home. Many gathered together so that there was no longer room for them, not even around the door, and he preached the word to them. They came bringing to him a paralytic carried by four men. Unable to get near Jesus because of the crowd, they opened up the roof above him.

After they had broken through, they let down the mat on which the paralytic was lying. When Jesus saw their faith, he said to the paralytic, 'Child, your sins are forgiven."
Now some of the scribes were sitting there asking themselves, "Why does this man speak that way? He is blaspheming. Who but God can forgive sins?" Jesus immediately knew in his mind what they were thinking to themselves, so he said, "Why are you thinking such things in your hearts?

Which is easier, to say to the paralytic, your sins are forgiven, or to say, rise, pick up your mat and walk? But that you may know the Son of Man has authority to forgive sins on earth," he said to the paralytic, "I say to you, rise, pick up your mat, and go home." He rose, picked up his mat at once, and went away in the sight of everyone. They were all astonished and glorified God, saying, "We have never seen anything like this."

Jesus was saying that actions speak louder than words and that he had the authority to do God's will. We too can accomplish great things through God and the Holy Spirit if we believe. Every summer a small boy went with a group of friends down to the creek where there was a swimming hole. The older boys would climb up a steep path to grab a rope that hung from a tree, allowing the bravest to swing out and jump into the water. The little boy had always been too scared to even attempt to swing, but he vowed one year that he would gather together enough courage to jump from the swing into the creek.

As he climbed up toward the swing to fulfill his vow, his nervousness increased but he managed to make it all the way up to the top and grab the rope. After taking a few moments to gather his thoughts he stepped back and jumped off the cliff. He swung out over the water, but held onto the rope, swung back toward shore and slammed into the tree. He was injured so badly that he didn't try to jump again for the rest of the summer, but the next year he finally jumped off the shore.

Asked how he finally managed to jump, he said, "The secret to my success was learning to let go." The success of our lives and our relationship with God is based on the same fact: learning to let go in faith and be anchored in God. People may constantly try to tell us how to live and question our motives. After all, what authority, what right do we have to do anything? Only God has the authority and only God can prove anything. We have to get past our fear and doubt because we cannot see God. We must have faith. We are only the messengers, but if we are working for God, the fruit of our actions can be our proof.

One day a family was awakened in the middle of the night by the realization that their house was on fire. When the father made his way outside, he realized his young daughter was not with the rest of the family. He was just about to try and go back inside when he saw his daughter at the upstairs window. He called to her and told her to jump out of the window, but the little girl was panicky and frightened. She said she was too scared to jump. The father and the daughter argued for a minute until the father told her that the flames were going to get closer soon and she would have to jump out of the window. Just then, the little girl shrieked, 'I can't see you!"

"But I can see you." Her father replied, "And I will catch you."

We must trust in the fact that God can see us and will catch us; but we have to be the ones who make the leap of faith. Sometimes when we are motivated to give God a chance in our lives we can become inactive and paralyzed. We can sit back and allow things to happen to us, as if we're waiting for God to act but Jesus tells us to do the opposite. Our entire relationship with God should make us active. God's message is about doing, about how to put our beliefs into practice and apply God's love.

Actions

Actions are how we can exercise and express our faith every day. Parents often express frustration because their children don't have a relationship with God, but the best thing we can do for any of our children is show them the joy and purpose that God brings to our lives through our own actions. We can't expect anyone to feel anything we don't feel ourselves, and we can't expect people to do anything we don't do ourselves. We teach not by what we say but by our example. We model our faith by what we do.

From another person's perspective, it is more important for us to act as God wants than to talk about what God wants, but our faith is our personal reason. As we put larger and larger crosses around our necks, tattoo religious symbols on our bodies and put vanity plates and bumper stickers on our cars proclaiming our love of Jesus, we must ask ourselves why those badges are there. Are they a kind of trophy for other people to see? Faith is our reason, but actions are our proof of God to others.

Faith is not a spectator sport, nor is life. Our relationship with God should be shown through our actions. In a letter of Saint James (2:14 - 18) he writes:

> *What good is it, my brothers and sisters, if someone says he has faith but does not have works? Can that faith save him? If a brother or sister has nothing to wear and has no food for the day, and one of you says to them, "Go*

in peace, keep warm, and eat well, but do not give them the necessities of the body, what good is it? So also faith of itself, if it does not have works, is dead." Indeed someone might say, "You have faith and I have works." Demonstrate your faith to me without works, and I will demonstrate my faith to you from my works.

The sort of acts one might be called on to do is act just as Jesus would in our situation. Jesus instructed his disciples to clothe the naked, to feed the hungry, and to heal the sick because in doing so we are doing so for God. When thousands of people were with Jesus in a deserted place, the disciples told him to let the people go off so they could find something to eat in nearby villages. Jesus told them to "Give them some food yourselves." When the disciples replied that all they had were five loaves and two fish, Jesus asked the intercession of his father in Heaven to multiply the meager supplies and Jesus was able to feed five thousand people until they were full. Twelve wicker baskets held what was left over.

Jesus put pressure on the disciples to take care of the problem themselves, then made sure that their effort was more than enough. Through this miracle he tells us to take care of problems by ourselves. He reminds us that we will be given whatever we need as long as we have faith. Whatever we do for the benefit of others God will make sure it is not only enough but more than enough. Our only job is to try.

In the Bible, good works are the measure of faith-fulness to God. Entrance to Heaven is based on the merit of our lives, not because of who we are but because of the love and service we show. Our faith can be our trophy, the image, or faith can be the means to make God clearer to us through service programs, food-drives, clothing drives or volunteering at the soup kitchen: the most common ordinary tasks made exceptional.

Seeing the Possibilities in People: Heroes

The people in our lives that we consider our heroes may be sports figures, politicians, entertainers, or business magnates. We might want to have their fame, their influence, accomplishments, or fortune; but we probably don't know anything about them person-ally. When public revelations that Michael Jordan and President Kennedy compromised their integrity and had extramarital affairs, or that Michael Jackson has been accused of molesting juvenile boys, do we care? When our heroes are shown to have committed a crime, exposed a dependency on drugs or alcohol, exhibited some destructive behavior or shown a lack of integrity because of a weakness in their character, does it matter to us?

Are they no longer heroes to us when we find out about their failings? The big question is why did we look up to them in the first place? Who are the real heroes in our lives and what did they do?

The following email was sent around the Internet several years ago:

1. Name the five wealthiest people in the world.
2. Name the last five Heisman trophy winners.
3. Name the last five winners of the Miss America contest.
4. Name ten people who have won the Nobel or Pulitzer Prize.
5. Name the last six Academy Award winners for Best Actor or Best Actress.

How did you do? The point is, none of us remembers the headliners of yesterday. These are not second-rate achievers. They are the best in their fields. But the applause dies. Awards tarnish. Achievements are forgotten. Accolades and certificates are buried with their owners, and trophies ultimately don't count for much.

Now here's another quiz. See how you do on this one:

1. List the teachers who truly aided your journey through school.
2. Name three friends who have helped you through a difficult time.
3. Name five people who have taught you something worthwhile.
4. Think of five people who made you feel appreciated and special.
5. Think of five people you enjoy spending time with.
6. Name a half-dozen heroes whose stories have inspired you.

Easier? What's the lesson here? It's that the people who make a difference in your life aren't the ones with the most credentials, the most money, or the most awards.

They're the ones who care.

We decide what is important to us and we decide who is important to us. Our heroes gave us their attention and made us feel important; they made us feel special. They made us feel as if we really mattered, like the parents, teachers, friends, and coaches on our list above. They weren't perfect, but they did something great for us. They gave us their time and were there for us at some moment in our lives when we needed them. They acted as if there was nothing else they would rather be doing and no one else they would rather be with in a moment when we needed help.

A woman I know named Liz had a special hero: her seventh grade English teacher, Mrs. Scott. The teacher stayed after school to talk to Liz, who often felt ignored at home and with classmates. Mrs. Scott encouraged Liz to put her thoughts and feelings down on paper, and supported Liz and her attempts to write. As Liz grew older, she often returned to her grade school to seek out Mrs. Scott's advice and encouragement. A writer today, Liz says she owes her love of writing to the woman who first took her work seriously.

Bob Dylan wrote, "A hero is someone who understands the responsibility that comes with his freedom." A hero is someone who helped us *when we needed help*. We all have problems and flaws but we can all be heroes to others if we do what others have done for us: show love. God asks us to behave in such a way that we belong on other people's lists of heroes.

During the horror of the 9/11 terrorist attacks countless individuals performed heroic deeds. Firefighters and policemen ran *up* into the burning World Trade Center towers to save people as others were running out. Passengers on the hijacked plane that crashed into the Pennsylvania countryside rushed the hijackers and gave their lives to keep the plane from reaching its intended target, thought to be the White House. They spared many people's lives by confronting the terrorists on the plane. Those individuals showed incredible strength to sacrifice their lives for other people. They thought of other people more than they thought of themselves. There's no trophy involved with these examples at all, simply care and concern shown to others in need, and a warm place in the hearts and memories of many Americans.

CHAPTER FOURTEEN

What we control: actions and reactions

I f we claim our relationship with God as our own, we gain a certain amount of control. Conversely, claiming that predestination and fate rule our lives assumes that we have no control over what happens to us. It's easy to say, "Okay God, I'll give you a chance, I'm being receptive to you, go ahead and do what you do," but acknowledging God does not mean God is responsible for what happens to us. We can't sit back and wait passively for God; we must work actively to reach God. The gift of free will enables us to take an active role in our lives through the decisions we make. If we say that God gave us free will but doesn't want us to use it, that doesn't make sense. We must decide whether we get closer to God or not.

As Scott Peck writes in *People of the Lie*: "There are only two states of being: submission to God and goodness, or the refusal to submit to anything beyond one's own will. We must ultimately belong to God or to the devil."[28] Assuming that we have ruled out a life of evil, we must actively choose to belong to God. There is no such thing as neutral territory.

Those of us who feel that our lives are out of our control forget how much say we do have in the direction our lives are going through the decisions we make every day. We decide what clothes we wear, what we eat, whom we are friends with, and what our bedroom looks like. Children are often forced against their will to go to family functions at Christmas and Thanksgiving, to visit friends of the family they don't want to see, and to attend school. One of the best things about getting older is having the freedom to choose what we do and be able to decide for ourselves to avoid uncomfortable situations.

When the president of a high school announced his decision to leave, a flier was distributed to all the teachers asking for donations for a good-bye gift for him. One experienced teacher reacted to the letter by throwing it in the trash can. He was annoyed at the request because he knew that the president was making a very good salary and was leaving under mysterious circumstances. He simply did not see the importance of giving a pen or wallet to a man who probably had a better one.

Instead, he thought of the cafeteria workers. The café ladies never received any recognition or thanks for the job they did, even though every day they did the best they could, including putting up decorations in the café and dressing up in costumes for Thanksgiving, Halloween, and Christmas. The teacher decided to go buy a bouquet of flowers and deliver it to the cafeteria to thank the ladies for their efforts and let them know they were appreciated. He continued to do that every year while he was at the school. The teacher's decision was to make a difference in the lives of the people he came in contact with every day, and he saw that as a reflection of his relationship with God. He realized that we do control our actions and reactions to situations in our lives and the decisions we make are under our control.

Assuming control of our lives: Decisions

While growing up we may drink excessively, take drugs, or allow ourselves to be sexually promiscuous, but we do make decisions. Ultimately we either make decisions in our own best interest or not. Either we put ourselves into uncomfortable situations or we avoid them. One sign of growing up and being mature is being responsible enough to make good choices and decisions, like avoiding a party where we know there will be drinking and drug use if we don't want to be around alcohol or drugs. Let's say that we are teenagers in high school in a class with everyone we know. The teacher asks, "If you drink, or have had alcohol, go stand on this side of the room. Everyone who hasn't, stand on the other side of the room."

If the question were asked about sex, drugs, cheating, lying, or other facets of our character, would we try to hide behind others because we would be embarrassed about which side of the room we were on? Would it matter which side of the room we were on as long as we were with the cool people, or would we lie, deny the truth and go to the side where we didn't belong?

Being asked all those questions would force us to be responsible for our decisions, whether we told the truth or not and we might be proud or ashamed of the side we were on. We might also be surprised which side of the room other people were on. We should consider why we care so much about what other people think of us. We might spend much of our time worrying and caring about what other people think of us while we are in fact responsible for our own lives. We should be more concerned about which side of the room we're on.

Speaking of decisions, no civilization in history has the amount of food available to its citizens that the United States does. With 30%, or approximately 1 in 3 Americans being obese, it is obvious that we Americans not do make healthy choices. Some people have even sued fast food restaurants for making them overweight rather than take responsibility for their dietary and health decisions. Every large super-market carries 100's of types of shampoo, and over 80 different types of painkillers, not to mention the dozens of candy, chip, and soda choices available.

Drugs, especially marijuana and alcohol, have been around for millennia. Whether as a kid in school or as an adult we have to decide whether to drink alcohol or not, and if so, how much. Do we want to? When drugs are offered, do we take some, or can we say no? How do we know whether to smoke pot and drink or not? We also wonder if other people will think we're not cool if we refuse. It's easy to make a fool of ourselves, be stupid and make mistakes by drinking too much or allowing drugs to take us away from reality and put us into fantasy.

How are we supposed to deal with sex? Dealing with our sexual urges, desires and our sexuality is a struggle every person is faced with at some point. How do we determine our limits regarding sex? We've given sex a bad name because we've made it a narcissistic activity. Take pornography for instance, which turns sex from a total physical and emotional participatory experience into a recreational spectator sport, a spectacle instead of an activity of total sharing, giving and vulnerability. If sex is selfish it really doesn't matter if we have a partner or not; it's all about self-pleasuring.

Sex that is self-gratification can make us see people as conquests or trophies. Sex with a partner but without emotional involvement on our part might feel unfulfilling. If sex includes concern for another person, it becomes an expression of that concern and involves a completely different kind of feeling.

Sex is a giving, sharing part of a healthy, committed relationship if it is not only about us but includes commitment to the other person. That is what the commitment of marriage represents. Our morals and values weigh upon us. Our conscience is our guide, and what our family, church, friends, and society tell us all goes into the decisions we make regarding sex. But we alone, personally, and individually, set the limits and parameters of our sexual behavior through our decisions.

If little kids wet their pants, that's an accident. As we get older we are supposed to learn control. If a child keeps wetting his pants, he has a problem and must get help for it but he might not be able to help himself. We might have a problem with drugs, alcohol, relationships, sex, honesty, or many of life's decisions and conditions. If we keep making decisions we can't control and which harm us, we can't try to hide from them and ignore them; we have to fix those problems that we in essence create for ourselves.

Sex can make us feel pleasure for a few minutes, and drugs or alcohol make us feel good for a few hours by taking away feeling, removing pain, distracting and anesthetizing us until the effects wear off and we discover that the pain is still there. So we reach for the bottle or the drugs or use sex again in a desperate attempt to mask that pain.

Casual sex, drugs, and alcohol are temporary, and the guilt, depression, regret, and/ or embarrassment that accompanies them comes at a price. They make us momentarily feel good by numbing us so we don't feel anything, or deceiving us into delusions and feelings that the "high" is the reality. They are temporary escapes which deaden us and let us hide for a moment in fantasy, the opposite of being more aware. Drugs, sexual activity, and alcohol also kill people. Alcohol was involved in 41% of fatal car crashes in the United States in 2001 and 2002 (17, 419 in 2002), and each fatality was estimated to cost society $950,000. [29]

Because the feelings of relief from sex, drugs or alcohol are temporary, they let us down. God can make us feel good about ourselves and our lives without hurting us. The good feeling God brings us is permanent and causes no negative side effects, isn't deceiving, doesn't harm us or others, and brings us closer to real life instead of taking us away from it.

Fitting in socially, being accepted, and accepting ourselves are major concerns for all of us. God is available to help us with decisions which are just too personal to share with a friend or parent. God can help us steer our way through the minefield of sex, drugs, alcohol dependency or character issues such as greed, deceit, and selfishness covered by the Ten Commandments and God can help us clarify the questions we want answers to, even the ones too personal to share with anyone else.

God can help us find answers to those questions and help us deal with our stresses, concerns and pressures. All we have to do is open the lines of communication between ourselves and God. We must admit, accept, and take responsibility for every single decision we make and realize that everything we do, every single decision we make has a consequence and defines us. Every decision we make also reflects our relationship with God.

The Door

God is with us, but we may have closed a door between us. It's revealing of God's nature that the most powerful force in the universe relinquished power so we can have some control over our lives. God doesn't fight with us to come into our lives but lets us use our free will to decide for ourselves whether we allow God inside our lives or not.

Imagine a door between us and God. God is right on the other side of the door, but the door only has a doorknob on our side and can only be opened from our side. God is knocking on the door but it's our choice, our decision to respond. We are the only ones who can open the door and let God in to be a part of our lives. There is a famous painting by Holman Hunt based on Revelations 3:20-21, which shows Jesus in a garden knocking at a large oak door. The caption reads, "Behold I stand at the door and knock." In our relationship with God we cannot be passive and expect God to open the door but actively turn the knob ourselves and let God in.

This door between us and God can take three forms. We can intellectually shut out God if we rationalize why God can't or doesn't exist; we can close ourselves off emotionally by refusing to risk being vulnerable and need God, or we can close ourselves off spiritually by refusing to admit that there is any other portion of life apart from what we can see. Once we shut any of these doors, our spirit, our concern with the part of our life we feel rather than usually see to experience, will be shut off and die.

We can imagine ourselves as blind, deaf, and mute. We must actively search for and feel around for God. If we open the door allowing ourselves to be open to God through our intellect and our feelings we will receive the heightened awareness to experience God through our daily grind. That is how we establish a relationship with God. We may never give God a try because we might not want to stop being self-absorbed and give up "control" of our lives. It's natural for us to be afraid. Our willful pride might keep us from trusting God or admitting we need God's help. Faith is not a question of finding God, having all the answers, or understanding everything; it's a question of being willing to open up and trust God. Surrendering to God is not losing control; it's how we take control of our lives and allow God to work through us. Matthew 8:2 - 3 says:

A man suffering from leprosy came to him (Jesus), knelt down before him, and said, "Sir, if you want to, you can make me clean." Jesus reached out and touched him. "I do want to," he answered. "Be clean!" At once the man was healed of his disease.

The leper did not plead or demand to be healed, the leper let Jesus decide. God *does* want to heal us if we allow it to happen and leave God in charge. Faith is our belief in God's power and direction. Sometimes trying to see God is like trying to capture sunlight in our hands: The more we try to isolate and locate the almighty, the more the Lord seems to elude us. Seeing

God is like looking through a microscope in biology class and trying to find an elusive microbe on a glass slide. We turn the knobs and everything is blurry when out of nowhere we see something. *There it is! No, it's gone. There it is again! No, that wasn't it.*

How are we supposed to know what we're looking for? We don't even have to go out looking for God, God is right here with us. Our whole life is a matter of deciding whether we want to focus and refocus on God. There is a real feeling of accomplishment when we locate the microbe on the slide and we get better at doing it the more we practice it. We get better at finding God in our lives the more we practice trying to find God in our lives. If we could see God, we would see the true meaning of our lives and the direction we should go to attain salvation.

At the school-wide Christmas mass for the more than fourteen hundred students of Denis J. O'Connell high school in Arlington, Virginia, Fr. Michael Taylor told of a man who was comfortable in every way but was longing for something more in his life. The man went to visit a monk up in the mountains. He told the monk he was looking for God. The monk took the man to a pool of water, grabbed him and dunked his head into the pool of water, holding the man's head under the water, yanking his head out, and pulling his head into the water again. When he pulled the man's head out of the water, he told the man his search for God must be like his desire to breathe, desperate and essential for the man to live. The man returned home and after several years went back to the monk, telling him that as much as he tried, he was never able to find God.

Once again, the monk took the man back to the pool, dunked his head under the water, held it there, pulled it out, and pushed the man's head under the water again. After he pulled him out of the pool, the man, gasping, said, "I know, I know, I must seek God like my breath, desperately." "No," the Monk replied, "You must realize as desperately as you seek air; that is how desperately God is attempting to contact you." God even sent his own son in an effort to contact us and explain God's form to us, and that love from God is what we call grace.

CHAPTER FIFTEEN

Grace

The definitions of grace found in Webster's dictionary include: freely given unmerited favor and love from God; virtue of divine origin; condition of being in God's favor; and mercy or clemency. Roget's thesaurus lists kindness, elegance, blessing, and to dignify as words being similar in meaning to grace.

Grace is both a noun and a verb. If grace is unmerited favor, does that mean we are undeserving? We didn't earn God's grace through anything we did; God provided grace to us as a gift. Because we are sinners and imperfect, we don't deserve unconditional love, and we can't justify being cocky, arrogant or conceited. However, if we believe we have been formed by the ultimate power in the universe to perform an important job, we are deserving of all the grace we have been given.

We are special because the God in us is special. Human nature is imperfect but our spiritual nature, the structure of God in us, is perfect. To reconcile how we can be imperfect sinners and be perfect and holy at the same time, we can remember that God is in us and say, "The God in me is perfect."

Catholic teaching says grace is obtained and earned through the Sacraments and good works. Protestant teaching says grace is already given to us and that we are saved by grace alone. As representatives of religious theology and philosophy debate the what, where, how, and when of grace within the Christian framework, if grace is God's freely given love, then we are constantly surrounded by and swimming in a state of grace right now. We must only discern how God is trying to get our attention. Our only task is to become aware of how that grace surrounds us.

First love

Whether we are trying to love ourselves or feel God's love, grace, we have to know what love is. If we know what love is, we must have felt love. Someone, somewhere, must have loved us, whether it was a spouse, parent, coach, teacher, friend or stranger. Something that this person said or did affected us and made us feel important. Any insecurity we have might initially make us wonder why anyone would love us. The idea that someone would see us as we are and still consider us worth loving is disarming because we are all insecure and imperfect.

By questioning others' motives, we begin to search for answers like the child who wants to know why the sky is blue. We can allow ourselves to believe, or at least consider the possibility, that we are loved because God finds us worth loving. That first little bit of grace given to us saves us and is the seed of love planted inside of us.

Frederick Buechner wrote:

"The grace of God means something like: Here is your life. You might never have been, but you are because the party wouldn't have been complete without you. Here is the world. Beautiful and terrible things will happen. Don't be afraid. I am with you. Nothing can ever separate us. It's for you I created the universe. I love you. There's only one catch. Like any other gift, the gift of grace can only be yours if you'll reach out and take it. Maybe being able to reach out and take it is a gift too."

Focusing on how to find grace in this moment brings us back to our ability to see beyond what is visible. Grace, our connection to God, is not like an Internet connection that we have to connect to and dialup. Our line to God is always on and we're always hooked up. Through grace, God and heaven are available to us here and our only job is to discern how.

Being Saved

The 1998 movie *Saving Private Ryan* documented a World War II incident in which a special military force was sent to bring home Private Ryan, the last remaining brother in a family whose three other sons had been killed in battle. The effort made by the group to reach the man ended up costing several of the men their lives. When they finally reached Private Ryan, the leader of the group, Captain Miller, told Private Ryan to, "Earn this."

Years later Private Ryan returned to the cemetery to pay his respects to the soldiers who gave the supreme sacrifice to save him. He collapsed and broke down in tears wondering if he had in fact lived his life in a way to earn or justify what was done to save him. He wondered why he had been chosen, recognizing the overwhelming reality that he was singled out and rescued at tremendous cost.

We are like Private Ryan. The ultimate sacrifice has been made for us and we have been rescued. A person can show no greater love than to lay down his life for another. Jesus died to forgive our sins and bring us salvation. We must evaluate our lives in the same terms Private Ryan did, wondering if we justify the effort made to save us. God does not tell us to earn our salvation: it is given freely. God *is* out to get us; not to punish us, but to pick us up and lead us to salvation.

God is not a stalking hunter trying to inflict pain and punishment on us, but a rescuer attempting to save us and take us home. Upon acknowledging that

God is a relentless pursuer who is not a predator but a benefactor and a sponsor, our response can only be overwhelming gratitude at the realization of what was done on our behalf. We have been saved through God's love and been given the gift of salvation.

Our search for God is a circular route. The love God has shown us is the catalyst- the energy necessary to start the search for meaning which is a continual process. God's love, our potential to love and our role in this life begin to make sense to us if we realize we were rescued at great expense and for a reason. We were deemed worth saving by God because we have a job to do. We have to create God's kingdom.

God loves us even though we can not believe it. All we have to do is be ourselves. We might start paying more attention to our potential if we admit we are loved by God, but what an ideal situation! God loves us as we are and remains constantly in love with us, setting us free and allowing us to be ourselves. Maybe God does more than love us. Many of us love pizza but we wouldn't give up our life for a piece. Jesus died for us to show how much he was in love with us. God is our biggest advocate and we should be important to ourselves because we are important to God and God knows who we are. God knows our name.

God knows our name

God saved us from a life that ends, God loves us and we can even communicate with God. As opposed to a one-way attempt to contact an indifferent and inattentive Savior, we can make our relationship with God personal and active. Christians believe that we can not only communicate directly *to* God, but that we can communicate *with* God.

In an attempt to attract the attention of their idol at a rock concert teenage girl's wave, tremble, scream, and even cry, reaching an emotional frenzy. They long to have an autographed photo of their idol, but that is not personal interaction. The performer does not know them as individuals and that is one-way communication. God knows who we are. God constantly attempts to get our individual attention, and it is we who need to acknowledge God and communicate back.

A friend of mine who teaches high school can easily spot the most popular kids in class: They crave attention. She can also spot the timid, shy, insecure kids who no one else notices, they try to avoid attention. Students in most classes don't even know the names of classmates, just as many adults don't know the names of work associates or neighbors.

In every class that my friend teaches she assigns seats, even to seniors, so she can learn student names quickly. She says the names of each student in class out loud and points to where they sit so everyone can see their faces. The teacher plays a game in which she asks a student to identify by name three or four classmates the teacher chooses and if they get the names correct, the students get a couple of pieces of candy.

She embarrasses those who resist learning other people's names by accusing them of being snobbish or thinking they are too good to care about their classmates.

Eventually they all participate, and she plays the game until everybody knows everybody else in class. For insecure teenagers, isolation and rejection contribute to their feelings of worthlessness. God knows our name and thinks we're important. God knows who we are and we have God's undivided personal attention. That should make us feel important.

The Missing Commandment

Admitting that God has a clear view of us and loves us can lead us to pursue a relationship with God feeling valuable, wanted, and loved. A relationship is not a war or competition, but can become this way if we think of protecting ourselves too much. The spirit of a relationship should not be restrictive. In a tug of war we try to pull away from each other to move the ribbon in the center of the rope over to our side so we win. Two people in a relationship shouldn't be pulling apart. They should both be going in the same direction, trying to get closer together.

Romans 13:9 says, "You shall love your neighbor as yourself." A second grader on the playground during recess does love other people just as she loves (or does not like) herself. If that eight year old were told that the coolest, cutest, most popular boy in class liked her it would probably cause her a lot of emotional stress as she worried about how she could justify that affection.

She might wonder why he liked her and even if he would still like her if he really got to know her because she wanted to make sure he only saw her good qualities. She might wonder how she should act so he would continue to like her. Second graders need validation and use relationships to define themselves. As adults, we also need validation. We need to know that we are loveable, that we matter and that we have value.

The commandment to love ourselves, which is not on the list of the Ten Commandments, may change our perception of the list. Honestly looking at our personal insecurities and limitations makes it easy to devalue ourselves and feel depressed. Religions like Catholicism constantly remind us that we are sinners, and after hearing this so often we can begin to feel as though we are bad and worthless, but, the worst disservice we can do is to degrade ourselves and expect God to fix us.

If we cut ourselves down we take no responsibility for our lives and expect God to change all our imperfections. In grade school, I knew a boy named Tom who was always teasing and bullying other children, often to the point of hurting them. Tom's alcoholic father died in a drunk driving accident and Tom tried to hide his embarrassment and anger by torturing others.

Causing pain and making people feel fear made him feel strong and in control. He hid his vulnerability by pointing out the flaws of others and did his best to make everyone feel as miserable as he felt himself. Insecurities and imperfections sometimes make us hate ourselves and alienate ourselves from other people. Isolation and selfishness cause pain for us and others. While few of us are bullies like Tom, all of us try to find ways to hide behind masks or distract ourselves from facing our problems.

Being too self-centered and self-absorbed can make us question our worth. People who inflict pain do so because of their own personal pain. Children tell their classmates they're fat, ugly or stupid because they are in pain and don't want anyone else to be happy. Adults and parents often tell children that they're disappointed in them if they don't fulfill the parent's expectations. A period of intense physical pain, such as breaking an arm or suffering from a severe flu, leaves us preoccupied with our personal pain and there is, at least temporarily, no room in our awareness for anything else but our pain. Emotional pain can also preoccupy us.

On an airplane, before the flight, the attendant demonstrates how, if there is a loss of cabin pressure, an oxygen mask will be released from the ceiling. Then they say, "Put your own mask on before attempting to assist anyone else." The same applies to our lives. We must love ourselves to be strong enough to love anyone else. Seeing ourselves as loveable can remove the emotional pain and feelings of insignificance, relieve our insecurities, and allow us to focus our attention outward on other people.

The Golden Rule is more of a prophesy than a request. We will in fact love others in the same way we love and respect ourselves. Admitting that God loves us can lead us to realize we really are worth loving, and when we love ourselves we can start loving other people. We must love ourselves, not as if we're perfect or in a cocky or arrogant way, but because God has saved us, forgiven us and given us salvation. If we see ourselves as God's vessels placed on this earth as builders, then we are very special beings, worthy of love, and we should be proud of ourselves and our potential.

Huston Smith wrote, "The supreme evidence of his (Jesus') humility is that it is impossible to tell what Jesus thought of himself. He was concerned with what people thought of God-God's nature and God's will for their lives."[30] Maybe Jesus, Mother Theresa, St. Francis and all those individuals we hold in highest regard loved themselves and were so grateful for God's gifts of forgiveness and salvation that they focused all of their attention on sharing that love with others. Remez Sasson wrote <u>The Villager and the Happy Man.</u>

In a small village in the valley, there lived a man who was always happy, kind, and well disposed to everyone he met. He always smiled and had a kind and encouraging word to say whenever necessary. Everyone who met him left feeling better, happier, and elated. People knew they could count on him, and regarded him as a great friend.

One of the village dwellers was curious to know what his secret was, how could he be always so kind and helpful? How is it that he held no grudge towards anyone and was always happy?

Once, upon meeting him in the street he asked him: "Most people are selfish and unsatisfied. They do not smile as often as you do; neither are they as helpful or kind as you are. How do you explain it? "When you make peace with yourself, then you can be in peace with the rest of the world. If you can recognize the spirit in yourself, you can recognize the spirit in everyone, and then you find it natural to be kind and well disposed to all.

If your thoughts are under your control you become strong and firm. The outer mask of the personality is like a robot programmed to do certain tasks. Your habits and thoughts are the programs. Be free from this programming and then the inner good that resides in you will be revealed."

"But a lot of work is necessary. Good habits have to be developed. The ability to concentrate and to control the thoughts has to be strengthened.

The work is difficult and endless. There are many walls that need to be climbed. It is not an easy task" Lamented the villager.
"Do not think about the difficulties, otherwise that is what you will see and experience. Just quieten your feelings and thoughts and try to stay in this peace. All the abilities and powers awaken spontaneously. You do not work on them directly. They are by-products of your peace of mind. Just try to be calm and do not let yourself be carried away by your thoughts."

"Is that all?" Asked the villager. 'Try to watch your thoughts and see how they come and go. Stay in the quietness that arises. The moments of peace will be brief at first, but in time they will get longer. This peace is also strength, power, kindness, and love. When you realize that you are one with the Universal Power, you will begin to act from a different dimension, not from the selfish, small, limited ego."

"I will try to remember your words," said the villager and continued, "there is another thing that I am curious about. You do not seem to be influenced by the environment. You have a kind word to everyone and are helpful. Yet people do not exploit your goodness, and they treat you well." "Goodness and being kind do not necessarily point to weakness. When you are good you can also be strong. People sense your strength and do not impose on you. When you are strong and calm inside, you help people because you can and you want to. You then act from strength and not from weakness. Goodness can also go with power and strength, it is not a sign of weakness as some people erroneously think."

"Thank you very much for your advice," said the villager and went away happy and satisfied.

Love is a feeling which must be felt to be believed. Unless we feel it what others tell us about it will only seem like deception because we have no connection to it. Jesus is said to have condensed the Ten Commandments into the Golden rule, which is: Love your neighbor as yourself. We may need to alter the wording of the statement to "Love your neighbor as God loves you" which is more the focus of Jesus' teachings.

CHAPTER SIXTEEN

Our lives are a preparation for the kingdom

Religions differ in their concepts of the afterlife, but all assume some sort of continuation of our existence. Heaven may be the celebration, induction ceremony, post- game party or trophy we attain based on the outcome of the game, but living our life is how we attain that trophy. If life is the game that we are playing right now, we will be judged by our performance

In his book *World Waiting to be Born*, Dr. Scott Peck writes: "*There is a devastating psychological disorder that afflicts one or two percent of the population-compulsive histrionics-constant crisis. The far more devastating form of psychological disorder which afflicts approximately ninety-five percent of individuals-is that they fail to live their lives with a sufficient sense of drama. They do not wake up and realize the critical nature of their lives until it is often too late.*"[31]

If we wait until we have enough money to start a family or buy a house, wait until the kids are out of the house to slow down and pay attention to our daily routine, or wait until we get to Church to pay attention to God in our daily lives, we may never appreciate the possibility available to us to bring God into each moment. We should seize the opportunity to create God's kingdom from what is right in front of us right now. The Latin phrase "Carpe Diem" which means seize the day, is similar to the saying, "There is no dress rehearsal for life."

Today, we're here. This is it. This *is* all there is. If we keep looking somewhere else for meaning we will miss the only reality and opportunity we have available to us: the present. We can only participate in our lives through what we do. Ivan Turgenev said, "If we wait for the moment when everything, absolutely everything is ready, we shall never begin."

As we look for meaning in our lives we seem to be looking everywhere else but where we are. As we wake up and get ready for work, scramble to eat something, get dressed and get ready to leave, God can't be there. As we pack the lunches for school or take the kids to practices, God can't be there, either. Thomas Mann, in *The Beloved Returns,* wrote, "Hold each moment sacred. Give each clarity and meaning, each the weight of thine awareness, each its true and due fulfillment."

Jesus tried to explain to his disciples how they could experience God in every moment, bring God to be a part of every interaction, and try to create Heaven. Jesus attempted to inspire the disciples to place more importance, more significance on every interaction. God was not hiding behind the curtain in the Temple where only the priest or Church elder could go, but where every individual could experience God: right here.

The disciples asked Jesus where God was and he told them, "In the least of my brothers and sisters." (Matthew 25:40). They asked Jesus what they could do for God, and he told them, "I was hungry and you fed me, thirsty and you gave me a drink." (Matthew 25:35). When they asked Jesus where the kingdom was, he told them, "It is among you but you do not see it." (The Gospel of Thomas 3:1 51, 113) Jesus seems to be saying the Supreme Being and the kingdom are both right in front of our eyes and not somewhere else but here. God is literally all around us in the grace available to us.

We continually evaluate and prioritize our life experiences and rate how important they are. We may believe the Most Valuable Trophy from our Sixth grade baseball team is our most prized possession and our wedding day, or graduation day are the most important days of our lives. We may also believe that God is in church and Heaven awaits us after we die.

Jesus' words and actions demonstrated that God's kingdom is not something we should be waiting for as if it will come later, but something we should be attempting to discern as if it is here with us now if we attach special meaning to every moment and bring God into it. He was telling us that there is more to the journey of our lives than just putting our heads down, staring at the ground and trudging toward our destination. Our job is to create God's kingdom among us now.

Where God is: Awareness

A six month old infant being held on an adult's shoulder looks around and becomes totally focused on who or what they're looking at. We may be shopping at the store and the child stares as if they're sucking information from what they're seeing. When they look at me and I look back it feels as if they're trying to see what's inside me. Their focus is complete and absolute. It's almost as if they're asking me with their eyes, "Are you nice or mean, happy or sad?"

Young children don't look at people or surroundings with subjective judgments or presumptions. Although they quickly form them, they don't have expectations; they're simply trying to find out more about what is around them. They are on a sincere, intense, fact-finding mission, and they are totally consumed by it. It is difficult for adults to look at others and their surroundings without judgment because preconceived notions and conditioned expectations alter our view.

In 1906 Russian Doctor Ivan Pavlov conducted an experiment where he rang a bell at mealtime for some dogs and found that after several repetitions, the dogs began salivating at the sound of the bell in anticipation of the food that would follow. This reflex also applies to our expectations and our conditioned response. Infants will open their mouths after tasting a spoonful of strained peas if they love them, anticipating the next spoonful. We expect God to be or act as we have been taught. Our goal to find God should be to view our environment like a clean, blank slate, simply being aware of our surroundings, what is visible and what is felt.

Awareness is the buzz word, the magic pill, the launch button that many books on spirituality discuss. Awareness is the basis for so many philosophies that we chase after it with reckless abandon, as if we are searching for a hidden treasure. Bumper stickers proclaiming, "I found it!" would have us believe that awareness is a one-time discovery and once we find it, we're done. Awareness is thought to be the answer, regardless of the question.

But what is awareness? To answer that, we must return to when, in 563 B.C., Siddhartha Gautama of the Sakyas clan was born in Nepal. Siddhartha became the Buddha, which means the "Enlightened One," or "Awakened One." His teachings of inner awareness were such that people questioned him about what he was. In a time of chaos, he seemed to be the only order.

"Are you a god?" They asked.
"No."
"An angel?"
"No."
"A saint?"
"No."
"Then what are you?"

Buddha answered, "I am awake."[32]

Maybe the Buddha was explaining more than we might think. Being *awake* means being conscious, aware and alert. His enlightenment did not label *who* he was as much as *what* and *how* he was. He lived in the moment, focusing his energies on understanding.

We can do the same by living more "in the moment" than we do. As we race to get through our everyday obligations, our day can become a blur and awareness of our surroundings may be passing by with it.

Struggling to find meaning in our lives and live one day at a time should lead us to take one step further and live one moment, one interaction at a time by trying to hear the sound, feel the temperature, and notice the smell of where we are at this moment. If we're looking anywhere else but here in the "now" we're going to miss awareness of the moment. Buddhists strive to live in the now and expand their consciousness to include and embrace every moment, past, present, and future.

Jesus tried to show the disciples how to attain a more heightened level of awareness, just as he challenges us today to do the same. Jesus' level of awareness is like that of a person who is sober in the company of drunkards and addicts on drugs. His awareness and consciousness is a different reality, a different spiritual place in the same physical place we are in right now.

As we look for meaning or accomplishment, we can miss too much of where we are by looking at our trophies for special meaning. For special meaning, we should place more importance on the possibility and potential of seeing God in this moment right here. How is God here? We bring God here through our love and awareness. We may be driving and blocking the access to the turn lane which is keeping four cars from turning. Simply by pulling up ten feet, we could allow all the cars to go, but our lack of awareness or lack of concern prevents us from doing so. When we open a door to God we keep it open through awareness and concern.

Searching for the Sacred: Spiritual Awareness

Hans Christian Anderson wrote *The Emperor and the Nightengale*, a tale of an Emperor who replaced a real, drab, bird with a golden mechanical bird. Almost too late he realizes the beautiful trophy cannot replace the relationship he has with the real nightingale, or provide moments of awareness, beauty, or peace which the bird provided.

The words *secular* and *worldly* refer to what is material, what we can see, hear, touch, taste or smell. "Sacred" means devoted to a deity or religious purpose, meriting veneration or great respect. Sacred means holy, blessed, and revered and usually has a spiritual meaning. When anything becomes so important to us that we deem it critical to our religious lives we may make it sacred. *Sacred* and *spiritual* refer to what we value, admire, hold in high regard and appreciate in the religious sense.

"Spiritual" is the opposite of "material." A thesaurus will give the words religious, holy, heavenly, and divine as words similar in meaning to *spiritual*. The words similar in meaning to *material* are fabric, substance, structure, foundation, and composition while *spirit* is connected to the unseen, the felt, and what else is part of our existence beyond what we can see. If we consider what in our lives has particular meaning, importance, and special significance, we think of what we hold sacred.

A relationship with God can make the unseen part of our lives (our spiritual awareness) become the foundation, the critical portion, the structure, composition and most important material of our lives.

Our spirituality is our attempt to understand the mystery of our existence and go beyond the trophy in our case to the effort and achievement it represents. Our spiritual awareness is our state of being, the value we assign to where we are and what we're doing. Our spiritual awareness is achieved through evaluating all the other facets of our environment. Our spirit is the knowledge of who, what, why, and how we are. Our spirituality is the one facet of our lives independent of the quantity and solely concerned with the quality in our lives.

As much as we consider our trophies as the substance of what we achieve, they are actually only the image. The substance of what we accomplish is inside of ourselves and what our trophies represent: our passion, our determination, our motivation, commitment, and courage. To begin the journey to spiritual awareness and satisfaction is to be aware of the source of the other portion of our existence beyond our sight, which is God.

Integrated Awareness

A book entitled *Powers of Ten* by Philip and Phylis Morrison shows illustrations from the perspective of the entire universe to the subatomic level, each picture ten times the size of the other. The book and internet site show how, as we change our perspective, we change how much of the world we see. From space it is impossible to see anything specific on the earth; yet, from the earth, as we focus on the trees and buildings around us, we cannot see the entire earth and are only able to see what is in our immediate vicinity. The saying of how we can miss seeing the forest for the trees is a reference to how we can miss sight of the whole picture by not shifting our focus from the specific to the general.

The pictures in *Powers of Ten* make up the whole from general to specific. One of the pictures shows all the stars in the solar system, and it is impossible to pick out the planet Earth. Another picture shows a man and a woman on a blanket in a Chicago park. We have to consider all the pictures together to understand the whole, because no one picture can show us everything. Each individual picture is a portion.

Zen Buddhism tells us to *be* the whole, to make ourselves one with the universe both specific and general, but how can we consider the portion we can't see? God is the means by which we connect the visible *here* to the spiritual, sacred, *there* portion of our life we can't see. We need to balance our perspective as we sit here trying to locate where we are now and find our place in the universe, but it's not as easy as just hoping it will happen. Both parts must be integrated.

Children under the age of three will eat until they are full, no matter how much food is on their plate. Older children will continue eating as long as there is food on the plate. The awareness of being full seems to be something we lose touch with as we get older. Trying to listen to our favorite song and notice the beautiful fall foliage of tree colors at the same time is difficult to accomplish. In the same way, it's impossible to see the entirety of our lives in each of our individual actions and interactions.

We can be more attentive to the specific awareness of Eastern beliefs as we head to general Heaven of Western religions through God. The days of our lives make up the pieces of this puzzle. We can get a better picture of how and where we fit into the puzzle by putting the pieces together. By doing this we can achieve a state called personal awareness.

Increased awareness is the experience of non-judging attention to the present like the awareness of a child. Attentiveness without any judgment is called "mindfulness," and is at the heart of Buddhist meditation. Buddhist meditation is being incorporated in many Judaic-Christian places of worship to people of many beliefs to increase their awareness.

Mindfulness is a resurrection of the concept of contemplative prayer and silent, deep, thinking.

This was a major element of early Christianity that gradually fell into disuse among the laity. Meditation, thought, reflection, or contemplation serves to increase our awareness and our concern from getting to the sacred Heaven of Western religions to being in the introspective, elevated sense of being which is central to Eastern schools of thought. This is one way to bring heavenly thoughts to earth and to have one foot on earth and one in heaven. Integrating Heaven and earth is accomplished by recognizing the relationship we have with both the spiritual and the visible.

CHAPTER SEVENTEEN

Finding God: Not exactly what we expect

Making the decision to allow God to be a part of our lives is a first step toward a relationship with God, but what are we looking for? The ancient dream of religious deliverance by the Jewish people called Millennialism was a concept of social transformation and perfect salvation but what does that mean to us personally? As the Jewish people awaited the coming of the Messiah, or Messiah's, Jesus Christ was born among them.

He was not the warrior they expected, nor did he wield physical strength to force people to do his bidding and follow him. Instead, he showed the people how to find peace and gave them a choice. He didn't take power away from people; he sought to give people power. He didn't use his power to organize a rebellion to overthrow the oppressive Roman government, but instead challenged the moral authority of the religious hierarchy in the Jewish Temple.

Jesus didn't lead an army. He lived without a home. His teachings weren't exactly what the Jews had in mind and the kingdom he spoke of wasn't the earthly kingdom they expected. Jesus was a commoner, one of their own, with no earthly power at all. It was as if there was no room for Jesus in that world. Even at his birth, there was literally no room for him in the dwellings of people, so he was forced to be born with the animals.

Maybe we keep Jesus out of our lives because he is not exactly what we have in mind and not what we are expecting. As we attempt to find God in our lives, our expectations should be that of a child, simply being receptive without placing any expectations on God.

Here, right now, wherever we are, God is trying to get our attention, but we may be looking in another direction. We may be trying to tell God what to do and where to be instead of accepting how God is with us. Our responsibility is not to figure out whether or not God is here with us, but *how* God is here.

A marriage won't work if one partner expects the other to change. A man who is a sloppy, lazy, philanderer may not be willing to become the neat and faithful mate his wife anticipates him becoming as she attempts to "change" him. Both parties are disappointed when expectations or obligations are placed on one another. Trying to change people from what they are to what they are expected to be creates those expectations and trying to place God into the constraints or limits of our expectations restricts God and expecting God to change to suit us does not work either.

We should be aware enough to judge objectively and evaluate events without prejudice.

Matthew 20, 1 – 16 states:

The kingdom of God is like a landowner who went out at dawn to hire laborers for his vineyard. After agreeing with them for the usual daily wage, he sent them into his vineyard. Going out about nine o'clock, he saw others standing idle in the marketplace, and he said to them, 'You too go into my vineyard, and I will give you what is just.' So they went off. He went out again around noon, and around three o'clock and did likewise.

Going out about five o'clock, he found others standing around, and said to them, 'Why do you stand here idle all day?' They answered, 'Because no one has hired us.' He said to them, 'You too go into my vineyard.' When it was evening the owner of the vineyard said to his foreman,' Summon the laborers and give them their pay, beginning with the last and ending with the first.'

When those who had started about five o'clock came, each received the usual daily wage. So when the first came, they thought they would receive more, but each of them also got the usual wage. And on receiving it they grumbled against the landowner, saying,

'These last ones worked only one hour, and you have made them equal to us, who bore the days burden and the heat.' He said to one of them in reply, 'My friend, I am not cheating you. Did you not agree with me for the usual daily wage? Take what is yours and go. Am I not free to do as I wish with my money? Are you envious because I am generous? Thus, the last will be first, and the first will be last.

We might react to God the same way as the laborers who worked all day reacted and expect more from God. What would *we* do the next day? Would we want to be hired last, knowing we would be given the same pay as if we had worked all day, or would we be thankful and go to work early to repay the kindness and good fortune shown to us? What would God do? If every worker would be treated equally, God might allow us to decide when we would go to work the next day. Then God would pay all laborers equally, as God had done the day before.

This story illustrates how our idea of justice and expectation might be very different from God's. God allows every one of us to decide for ourselves how we react. God doesn't think like we do, and more importantly, we don't think as God does. After all, God doesn't have a trophy case.

It seems that God only gets our attention when we get what we think we don't deserve, good or bad. Whether we get the job we wanted or the one our brother found for us at the fast food restaurant, God gets the praise or the blame. The lesson is for us not to place expectations on what God should do or how God should act, but to have faith in God, hope in God's kingdom, and appreciation and acceptance for what does occur in our lives.

Growing up I often heard people talk about how God entered their lives through some life-changing event which brought direction and focus to their existence. Even the people who spoke about a tragedy or other low point in their lives during which God came to them had something that I wanted; they had a relationship with God. I kept looking and waiting for some big event to change me and make God clear to me but it never happened. I had no clue where to look or even what I was looking for, but I wanted a relationship with God.

Even after I was married and had a son, I kept anticipating something big happening to me to show me where God was in my life. One night when my son was about two years old I was trying to sleep when I thought I heard a sound out in the hallway. It was the sound a ketchup squirt bottle makes when there's only a little ketchup left. I picked my head up off the pillow, waited, and after a few seconds decided it was nothing and laid my head down again. Then I heard the same sound again. I went out into the hall to see my son standing there with a pained expression on his face. He said, "Daddy, my belly hurts."

Being a good husband, I was going to let my wife sleep and take care of this myself so I told my son everything was okay and started to lay him on his back. He was still in diapers, and when I tilted him back, I might as well have been pouring water from a pitcher. Diarrhea covered the carpet and I yelled for my wife as loudly as I could. As I scrubbed the area and smelled the strong ammonia, I wondered where God was hiding and if God was amused.

A few years later after having a second son, I came home and found that he couldn't wait to share his day with me. He started filling me in as soon as I walked through the door. I was anxious to change clothes so I listened for a few minutes and then tried to head upstairs. My son told me he had to go to the bathroom but he wasn't done talking and he wanted me to stay with him until he was finished. He wanted to see me, or at least know I was there while he went to the bathroom with the door open. He made me stay within listening distance as he continued talking.

He was so small that to get on the toilet he would literally put his knee on the seat, climb up on the seat, stand up, walk around the back and straddle it, suspended. There he stayed for a good five minutes, talking nonstop. I kept asking him if he was done but he just said, "No" and kept talking. At that point I told him I really had to change my clothes but I would be right back. I ran upstairs and back down again where he met me in the hallway. His pants were still down. "Daddy, I pooped" he said. There it was on the carpet. Luckily it was all in one piece. As I cleaned it up, I wondered where God was and if the Almighty was laughing hysterically (the tears-in-the-eyes kind).

I was looking for God in some dramatic life-changing event marked by an obvious sign while I was going to work, cleaning, and babysitting the kids in the daily grind of the doo-doo of my life. God was trying to get my attention not in some major event or some abnormal situation, but in the normal, common, everyday situation that I was experiencing at that moment. God was trying to get my attention then and is still trying to get my attention in what I'm doing right now.

I finally figured out that God was even trying to get into my life in all those seemingly unsavory and supposedly meaningless situations that I ignored. God was trying to enter the world in every moment by how I responded to it and through the love I could bring to it. God may never give us our own big dramatic event, our personal little miracle, but since most of our time is probably spent in the normal and the routine anyway, maybe all we have to change is where and how we look for God. In the Bible in Kings I 19:9, 11-13: Elijah was told to go and look for the Lord.

Elijah came to a cave where he took shelter. Then the Lord said, "Go outside and stand on the mountain before the Lord; the Lord will be passing by." A strong and heavy wind was rending the mountains and crushing rocks before the Lord-but the Lord was not in the wind. After the wind there was an earthquake-but the Lord was not in the earthquake. After the earthquake there was a fire-but the Lord was not in the fire. After the fire there was a tiny whispering sound. When he heard

*this, Elijah hid his face in his cloak and went
and stood at the entrance of the cave.*

In that tiny whispering sound, God showed
himself to Elijah. God resides in those meaningless
little instances that make up our days, bringing importance to our lives and showing us those times aren't
so meaningless after all. Writing a check for $100
dollars can become a check for $1000 dollars if we
fail to pay attention to the placement of the decimal
point. Winning an Olympic championship may come
down to the thousandth of a second. Our challenge is
to bring God into the next interaction or conversation
with the next person we see by discerning how God
is there, and considering how we can bring God there
by paying attention to every detail.

Our Lady of Perpetual Help, a small Catholic
elementary school in the Hawaiian Islands, was
having severe financial problems. The school closed
for a day and sent the children off with the assignment to take a picture of God. The children returned
with pictures of fish, a landscape, a mother's hand
and many other photos that were compiled into a
book and published. The book brought the school
enough money to keep it open in perpetuity because
the students had found God, as we should, absolutely
everywhere around them.

When Jesus was born, God could have staged a
spectacle and made Christ's birth an extravaganza by
buying all the network television and cable network
time to get maximum publicity. God could have had
large screen TV's set up and made the birth quite a

media event to get attention. Instead, Jesus was born relatively unnoticed in a simple, unassuming fashion to a poor peasant family in a stable.

Martin Hanford created a character called "Where's Waldo" which is a cartoon with a man wearing a striped red sweater hiding in a page of artwork. The job of the viewer is to find where Waldo is among the other objects on the page. Waldo is hard to find because he doesn't stand out. On the contrary, Waldo blends in so much it's as if he's hiding. God may be blending in with our daily life so much that we can't find God, either, but finding God is similar to our finding Waldo. Once we find Waldo, we may wonder why we didn't find him sooner and our eyes seem to be drawn back to where Waldo is. Once we find God, we can find it easier to be drawn back to God in our daily life.

We may never get that big event in our lives in which to find God, but we have plenty of little ones. Maybe what's important isn't so much *what* we do to find God but *how*. Mother Theresa said, "God doesn't ask me to do great things, just little things with great love." Again, we're looking for a trophy or a trophy event; but God isn't in the trophy business.

Wanting to be somewhere else

Wanting to find God and meaning should lead us to look around, but where do we look? We can't be focused on our mission of obtaining awareness all the time but we have to make a conscious effort to pay more attention to this moment right now. On the quest to find what is important to us, everyday responsibilities can overwhelm us so much it is impossible to concentrate and pay attention to the task at hand.

If we can stop and enjoy being where we are, maybe we can start squeezing meaning and value out of what we're doing all the time and find God at the same time. Tomorrow never arrives, but today is always right here. We owe it to ourselves to celebrate the moment and our role in it. Maybe rather than being concerned with where we have to go or what we have to *do*, we should be more concerned with where we should *be*: more aware and involved in how we can bring God into this moment.

During a major snowstorm, I took my three kids to a nearby golf course to go sledding. It was very difficult for me to keep from saying, "Let's go home." My feet were freezing and I was worried about what degree of discomfort I was feeling instead of enjoying the moment. I was dying to get the heck out of there but instead of telling them we had to leave I considered how God would have wanted me to act, so I waited until they were so cold that they told me they wanted to go. I actually tried to see the situation from their perspective and stopped looking ahead and I became aware enough to let the moment happen.

That same week the kids and I went to shop at the grocery store, and once again I caught myself becoming impatient to get home. I let them do some shopping without getting antsy about leaving. These moments became examples for me of how ordinary activities were opportunities for me to try and act as Jesus would with my kids without hurrying to complete the task.

Eventually, we might have to come to the realization that the meaning or importance we're looking for is in the present. We can begin to understand we are where we should be all the time, even when we're stuck in what we think is the boring routine of our lives. Our challenge is to change our moments from common, normal and boring into uncommon, extraordinary, abnormal, and exciting environments because we have the potential to bring God into each moment by how we react to them.

CHAPTER EIGHTEEN

God is the interruption

As we consider the Western religion idea of *there* where meaning and importance are, we are still stuck where we are. The *here* or conscious awareness of Eastern religion is how we can connect the two places. Our awareness can be the bridge to cross from our spiritual to our physical location and back again, just as the Atlantic Ocean touches both its eastern and western shores. It is also a means for us to be open to the possibility of the sacred nature of every moment, activity, and interaction.

We look for God somewhere other than where we are, and when we try to look for value in our lives it often seems as though the world intrudes on us. People and things bother us and keep us from paying attention to what we're trying to do. Everyday obligations and errands, such as doing the laundry or cleaning the house, never seem to end and can overwhelm us. It's as if we're just about to sit down to dinner and the phone rings, or the baby starts crying while we're trying to talk on the phone. We may never be able to focus our attention on what we're doing because we're constantly being interrupted. But what if God is the interruption?

We hate interruptions and tend to be impatient when people or events distract us because we're concerned with our own agenda. But what if every interruption is a tap on the shoulder from God, asking us to slow down and pay more attention to our surroundings and play "where's God in this picture?"

As a minister was preparing an important sermon, he had a "Eureka moment" where the main points of his talk seemed to come together in his head. He anxiously anticipated getting the opportunity to sit down so he could put together an outline of the sermon, but first he had chores to attend to. His wife was out of town, so it was his responsibility to pick up the children from school, take his 9 year old daughter to swim practice, wash the clothes, clean the house, and prepare dinner.

By the time he picked up his daughter from her swimming practice, he had become so frustrated at not being able to work on his sermon that he began to get irritated. When his daughter got in the car and began talking to him on the drive home, he snapped at her that he was trying to finish his writing but he kept getting interrupted. His daughter became very quiet and felt guilty that she was keeping him from his important work. After a few moments of silence, she tearfully whispered, "I'm sorry, Daddy."

As soon as his daughter said that, the minister apologized for yelling at her. He told her that as much critical importance as he put on his sermon, she was more important to him than his sermon. He realized that the purpose of the sermon was to help him live his life; the purpose of his life was not to help him write his sermon. He said talking about God and his relationship with God should never take priority over actually bringing God into his life through his actions like picking her up from swim practice.

The minister ended up changing the emphasis of his sermon. He told his congregation that regardless of what they were writing, creating, or in the process of finishing, as important as their current project seemed and how critical the result might appear, God was every interruption.

The minister told his congregation that regardless of what we think, we don't have somewhere important to *go*, we have somewhere important to *be*: right here. Our attention must be focused to allow us to increase our level of awareness, involvement and enjoyment of this moment.

Gandhi said, "There is more to life than increasing its speed." An unknown author wrote, "Yesterday is history, tomorrow is a mystery, and today is a gift; that's why they call it the present." Both philosophers realized the pace of our lives is too fast, that we need to slow down to experience life as it is happening to us.

Our problem may be our lack of perspective. When the top is left off the toothpaste; when we get our sandwich with mayonnaise and onions (when we specifically asked for them to be left off); when we get interrupted by a child when we're right in the middle of a task, we react. We might do better to be thankful for having teeth, having food to eat, or especially the gift of having children instead of complaining.

Maybe our focus should be on the moment we are in rather than any time ahead or behind us. We have to stop wanting to be somewhere else and start wanting to be where we are. From God's perspective, we're where we should be all the time.

Getting Involved: How we react

In class at school, when we passively receive information, it may be hard to pay attention for long and focus on a specific topic. However, if we actively participate we usually have a better time and are much more likely to remember details and figure out the reason we are doing an activity. There are various learning styles and some people respond better to visual stimuli, while others respond to auditory stimuli. Our lives are the same-if we watch our life like a spectator, we can be passive and bored. If we participate, it becomes easier to get the point. Confucius said, "I hear and I forget. I see and I remember. I do and I understand."

A chemistry teacher gave each pair of students a paper clip as they entered the room on the first day of class. The students were then instructed to write down as many words as possible describing the paper clip. After a few minutes she made three columns on the board. The first column was for words describing how much of the substance there was, such as giving our height and weight on a resume. The second column was for descriptions of the object in regard to its physical appearance, or what it looked like. The third column was for words describing what the object did, or its behavior. The third column is the one that chemistry is concerned with: the behavior of material.

We can use that column to describe ourselves, too. Fortunately for us, we can voluntarily change our behavior, while elements can't. Although we preoccupy ourselves with what we look like and how many trophies we possess, Jesus never seemed to be concerned with anyone's appearance or lot in life. He was concerned with what was in people's hearts and with their relationship with God.

One afternoon some children were playing and their ball started rolling down a hill. When they began screaming and crying loudly, their father got upset with them. He explained that he was not upset that the ball went down the hill, but at their reaction. He was upset that they stood there watching the ball and crying.

The man told the kids that if they tried to go after the ball instead of passively watching the ball roll down the hill, they were at least trying to solve the problem. As we search for God we must keep the perspective to realize the possibility of finding God where we are. As we become aware of the many problems around us, we need to consider whether we are doing anything to solve the problem or just giving its victims our sympathy and remaining inactive, claiming that it doesn't involve us.

A little boy was with his family at a picnic under a shelter at a large regional park. It was a busy weekend at the park and people were everywhere. Carrying a bag of crackers with him, the little boy wandered over to another shelter where a very old woman was sitting at one of the tables. He sat across from her sharing his crackers and talking with her for a few minutes until he was called by his relatives to leave.

As he returned to his family, he told them he had been sitting with God. They laughed and told him that was great. At the same time, the old lady was being helped from the table where she was sitting, and she told her family that she had been sitting with God. Her family supportively told her that was wonderful and laughed as they put her in the car.

Maybe there is nothing to draw our attention to people or make us notice the people who we see every day, but could we say the same thing the little boy or the old lady did at the end of any of our days; could we take a picture of God today? If we ask God, "When did we see you among us?" we read in Matthew 25:31 - 41 that God would reply:

> *"I was hungry and you gave me food, I was thirsty and you gave me drink, a stranger and you welcomed me, naked and you clothed me, ill and you cared for me, in prison and you visited me.*

> *Then the righteous will answer him and say, 'Lord, when did we see you hungry and feed you, or thirsty and give you drink? When did we see you a stranger and welcome you, or naked and clothe you? When did we see you ill or in prison, and visit you?' And the king will say to them in reply, 'Amen I say to you, whatever you do for the least of my brothers, you did for me.'*

As it turns out, as Mother Theresa showed by caring for the forgotten poor of Calcutta, those people are not insignificant at all. They are the people to whom we should be ministering. They are as important as any other people in God's eyes. Those people right in front of us are the ones we must be aware of, not some other people somewhere else. Mother Theresa said those people are Jesus in disguise. We can find our own identity, our God clearly, and our connection to each other through assisting each other in this moment. We can connect our search for ourselves and our God through other people. An anonymous quote says, "I sought myself, but I could not see; I sought my God, but he eluded me; I sought my brother and I found all three."

The gospel tells of Jesus walking with the disciples as they quarreled among themselves about who would be the greatest among them in the kingdom of heaven. Jesus reminded them that whoever wanted to be first must be the servant of all the others. Whoever wanted to be exalted and get the big trophy from God must humble themselves in the service of others. Jesus told the disciples that real achievement is taking care of other people's needs. He told them that being first in God's eyes was like having a small child in our care. This message stresses the absolute importance of every moment and every interaction with every person.

Being first means being attentive and aware of what others need, just like caring for an infant. A small child has many needs requiring constant attention. There is nothing selfish about it. What a challenge, what an opportunity for us! God wants us to concern ourselves with those vulnerable and needy, like doctors and nurses who care for cancer or AIDS patients and the terminally ill. Not all of us can minister to the sick and dying, but we can all help the people around us. For those who want to do as God requests and serve those in need, luckily, all of us are in need in one way or another.

Sympathy

Sympathy and empathy are passive emotions we feel when we read the paper or watch the news and hear about a tragedy that does not directly affect us. We may think "That's too bad" or "What a terrible tragedy," then put down the paper or turn off the television, get back to our lives and forget what we just read or heard. We're so used to being shown tragedy in the media that we mentally turn the channel, rationalize our inactivity and end up doing nothing at all. The media programs us to receive information and attempts to keep our attention by compressing stories into a few seconds of information, but after presenting a tragedy, the media moves on to another story.

For example, if we are driving and see a man holding a cardboard sign saying, "Homeless, please help," what do we do? Sympathy makes us feel sorry for the person but cynicism makes us think he would just use the money for alcohol or drugs. We might wonder why welfare and aid programs aren't being used to help him. We may even mentally tell him to get a job, but we don't know anything about him or his situation. Do we simply ignore him until the light changes and we move on?

We can remain detached from a situation and pretend not to be involved by being a spectator, but how does our concern help the person? Telling people to eat well and stay warm without doing anything to assist them is passive, inactive sympathy. Compassion means to feel "with" someone and feel what they feel, and we can only do so if we are aware enough to put ourselves in their shoes.

Compassion leads us to act. When we demonstrate compassion, we consider how to best assist another person. One woman saw a homeless man holding a sign and told the man that rather than just give him money, she would take him into the fast food restaurant and buy him whatever he wanted. She wanted to help the man but wanted to make sure her assistance was used in the best interests of the man, not to buy him drugs or alcohol. We have resources to assist others, not just feel sorry for them or ignore them, but do what is in their best interest.

One winter morning I woke up to see what looked like some animals on the hill in our back yard. A few minutes later I saw my neighbor go out and start clapping her hands and waving at the animals to shoo them away. My wife, who noticed that the animals were dogs, took some food outside with our daughter to entice the dogs to our deck so she could check to see if they had any identification, which they did. Even though it was very early in the morning, my wife called the owners of the dogs. The people thankfully came and picked up their pets, which had been missing for two days.

We can ignore problems and rationalize our sympathetic inactivity, or we can put our relationship with God into action and attempt to get better at responding to the problems we see with compassion. Our lives are constantly interrupted and entered by others as we drive, shop, and work. We might work at cultivating compassion by working at ways to connect ourselves with, not disconnect ourselves from, the society around us. We can chase them away and shoo them out of our space, or we can be attentive and aware enough to make the effort to help them.

Homelessness, drug use and abuse, alcoholism, neglect and evil are in our communities and neighborhoods. We must do something about them. We can isolate ourselves or we can realize that every time we get mad at people or situations, when a car cuts us off, we lose our keys or we suffer the loss of a job, God is watching us to see how we react.

God is present with us through the tough times of our lives, the doubt, the sad moments, the death, illness, and tragedy. Perhaps we are pushed to see how strong our trust in God is through test after test, like Job was tested in the Old Testament. It's easy to be strong when things go well, but we will define ourselves by how we respond when our lives are at their worst.

A US Air Force World War II B-17 Bomber Pilot's wife had her fifth child and was misprescribed medication which left her paralyzed from the waist down after the birth of the baby. When friends and family acquaintances asked the Major if he was going to take legal action to seek monetary remuneration to make the government pay for the mistake, the Major replied, "If it would make my wife walk again, I would." He dealt with the tragedy by keeping his faith in God and not seeking retribution.

Through trials and doubt we are forced to either accept our life as it is or do something to change it, especially when people show hostility, anger, selfishness or lack of compassion. As we consider getting closer to God, are we watching someone else play the game of life, or are we playing ourselves? The truth is that the world's problems are not someone else's problems: they are ours.

A story by David Wolpe tells of a man who complained continuously about how terrible everything around him was. He couldn't believe God could allow all these problems to happen and not send anyone to help. He received this reply: "God did send someone to help; God sent you." We are God's workers. We have all heard the saying, "If you want anything done right, do it yourself" and we are all God has. Awareness can help us realize the responsibility we have to respond, to act, and to react to God so we can do God's will as Jesus did.

In World War II the bombing of the Allies and the Germans caused a great deal of destruction to a church. The faithful did their best to reassemble the structure, and even fashioned new stone to replace the broken ones until the church was repaired. Even the large statue of Jesus was placed in front of the entrance of the church. But the bombings had broken off the hands of Christ from the statue. After much deliberation it was decided not to replace the hands of the statue. Instead, it was decided to change the inscription of the statue to read, "I have no hands, but yours."

CHAPTER NINETEEN

God's will.
What should we do?

God is the smartest, richest, most powerful force in the universe who we may believe doesn't need us. If we believe God can stay at the presidential suite at the most luxurious hotel in the world and enjoy an endless all-expense paid vacation and therefore does not need us, then we are not important and our lives don't matter. But if we believe God has created a world and universe to share the experience and perfection of heaven with mankind, then God does need our help. God needs our help to create that kingdom.

In the book *The God Memorandum*, Og Mandino wrote that God tells all of us, "You need me, and I need you" and the reason is to make God's kingdom a reality and establish heaven on earth. God can only reach others through us. We are the physical link between God and other people, the way to connect heaven to earth. We are God's eyes, ears, hands, feet, and heart. God is the coach who needs us to perform an assignment for the team and we are essential. We are the laborer, the bridge between Heaven and earth.

Putting our spirit in God's hands can lead us to ask what God wants us to do.

Luke 3:10-14 says:

"The crowds asked John the Baptist, 'What should we do (to enter the kingdom of heaven)?' He said to them in reply, "Whoever has two cloaks should share with the person who has none. And whoever has food should do likewise.' Even tax collectors came to be baptized and they said to him, 'Teacher, what should we do?' He answered them, 'Stop collecting more than what is prescribed.' Soldiers also asked him, 'And what is it that we should do?' He told them, 'Do not practice extortion, do not falsely accuse anyone, and be satisfied with your wages.'

John told the people to simply do what they could to help the needy by giving food and clothing to those who had none and stop sinning against others, the tax collector by taking only what was his, and the soldier by not threatening others. Jesus said that doing what we could for the least of our brothers or sisters was doing what we could for God.

Candles

Edith Wharton wrote; "There are two ways of spreading light-to be the candle or the mirror that reflects it." God is the candle and we can be the mirror of God on earth. Let's say that one day we wake up to discover that we are candles in a candle factory. We are told by other candles that we are a candle. We look around and see we're candles, but we don't even know what a candle is. We're just one of many. We wonder if we really matter. Then someone lights us. We feel the heat and warmth we generate and see the light we give off, and we start to understand. We're a candle, and our light is important.

We are important not because of what we are, but because of what we can do. We can define ourselves by what we can accomplish, not as trophies we accumulate but in terms of the heat, light, and warmth which we are able to generate. We have the potential to light up and provide light for others too. Our capacity and ability to give off light and warmth makes us important because we can love as Jesus did.

We can reflect the perfect light of God through our lives if we let it come out through us. Just as the candles did not know of their potential until they were lit, we do not know what we are or what we are capable of until we feel God's love for ourselves.

Gifts

Our life is a gift from God and what we do with it is like the Bible story of the workers who were given their boss's money. One invested wisely and made more money, one did nothing with the money, and one buried the money and lost what little he had. God expects us not just to hide or bury our talents and abilities but to develop them, use them and improve them. Our gift, whether it is musical genius or an uncanny ability to remember show tunes, may seem like the simple, hand-written note from a child to a parent, but being an unconditionally loving parent, God cherishes the works of art that come from our heart.

We have a function, a reason for being here, a part to play. We can contribute in creating God's kingdom. We have talents and gifts such as athletic abilities, musical talent, creativity in arts and crafts, writing ability, understanding of science and mathematics, or a gentle nature that makes other people feel comfortable and at ease around us. Those gifts make us unique. Leo Buscaglia wrote, "Your talent is God's gift to you, what you do with it is your gift to God."

In Corinthians I 12:4-11 it is written:

> *There are different spiritual gifts, but the same Spirit; there are different forms of service, but the same Lord; there are different workings but the same God who produces all of them in everyone. To each individual the manifestation of the Spirit is given for some benefit.*
>
> *To one is given through the Spirit the expression of wisdom; to another the expression of knowledge according to the same Spirit; to another faith by the same Spirit; to*

another healing; to another mighty deeds; to another prophesy; to another discernment of spirits; to another varieties of tongues. But one and the same Spirit produces all of these, distributing them individually to each person as he wishes.

A child may have a natural talent for singing, playing music, or athletics and may stand out when he is young. As he gets older, he may find that the most talented aren't always the most successful. The most successful are the ones who work hardest and who are the most competitive to improve whatever talent they have. The star basketball player who was Most Valuable Player of her seventh grade basketball team may lose her skill without constant practice, training, and exercise.

Even though God gives us a talent or gift, the focus isn't on us. Maybe we have a gift because we, from God's perspective, are the means to deliver that gift to other people. We have to give a task our best effort, then leave the rest to the Lord. The satisfaction of doing our best and running the good race is enough. Theodore Roosevelt wrote:

"It is not the critic who counts; not the man who points out how the strong man stumbled or where the doer of deeds could have done them better. The credit belongs to the man who is actually in the arena, whose face is marred by dust and sweat and blood; who strives valiantly; who errs and comes

short again and again; who knows the great enthusiasms, the great devotions; who spends himself in a worthy cause; who, at best, knows in the end the triumph of high achievement, and who at the worst, at least fails while daring greatly, so that his place shall never be with those timid souls who know neither victory nor defeat."

Being afraid of failure can keep us from participating, and sometimes even being afraid of success can keep us from participating. Anyone who hasn't suffered defeat hasn't competed, and the only way to be sure we won't fail is not to play. The times we bring God's love into the world are the very trophy's that will define our lives and give them meaning. Not only by stopping to help a motorist stranded in the snow, but in how we acknowledge the mailman or garbage collector is how we show God our faith and show others our faith in God. It may not be anything people would see on the evening television news, but it may be the picture of God for someone today.

Our Job

Saint Peter spoke of being all things to all people. Those words may seem cocky or arrogant to us but he meant that our job is to attempt to be whatever other people need us to be. When we see people in pain we should be compassionate, when people are weak we should be strong. In every situation we should act as

Jesus would by doing what's in the best interest of the individual. St. Francis wrote:

> *Lord, make me an instrument of your peace.*
> *Where there is hatred, let me sow love;*
> *Where there is injury, pardon;*
> *Where there is doubt, faith;*
> *Where there is despair, hope;*
> *Where there is darkness, light;*
> *Where there is sadness, joy.*
> *Oh divine Master, grant that I may not so much seek to be consoled as to console; to be understood as to understand; to be loved as to love; for it is in giving that we receive, pardoning that we are pardoned, and dying that we are born to eternal life.*

How strong do we have to be to do all that? Are we supposed to think about the needs of other people and try to take care of them instead of ourselves? As a matter of fact, we are, but not instead of ourselves but in addition to ourselves.

In the Parish Hall of a Catholic grade school hangs a panel from the comic strip Family Circus, which says, "You can give your kids things, or time. Time is better." A radio advertisement from the Church of Jesus Christ of Latter Day Saints stated that the most important gift parents can give to their children is their time.

If we think something in our relationship with our Lord, our kids, family, or friends is lacking, we should invest our time in order to correct the problem. The daily routine of job, school, work, and meals defines our lives in tiny pieces. We take pictures of vacations to remember great experiences, but what if we took pictures of today's mundane events. Is God in there anywhere and would we have good memories of it?

This story given as a sermon at a Catholic mass illustrates the nature of our "job." A daughter of seaport innkeepers met a sailor. The sailor seemed to be a good man and after several years and many visits, he became a family favorite. Then, on one visit the sailor asked the girl to marry him. She replied she was young and her parents needed her to manage the inn. The sailor was sad but he understood and promised that one day they would be together.

Years later the sailor came back and once again asked the girl, who was a woman now, to marry him. As she embraced him, she told him that her parents were old and in failing health and she needed to care for them and the inn. Again the sailor said he understood her obligation to her parents, but that one day she would go with him.

Several more years passed and the sailor returned again. When he saw the woman, she told him both of her parents had died and she was running the inn by herself. The sailor reminded the woman that her family no longer needed her and it was time for them to be together. She knew he was right, but she became nostalgic and overwhelmed thinking of how she had lived her whole life in that town.

The sailor understood how she felt and told her to take her time and think about her answer. He assured her that he loved her and would await her reply, but he said that he was also making changes in his life and would be leaving the next morning and not returning. The woman said she would give him an answer as soon as possible.

That evening, as the woman could think of nothing else but the sailor, she weighed her options and spent the entire night talking with her friends. Finally, she realized the sailor was right and she belonged with him. Knowing it was late, she made hasty preparations to go. While taking care of all her affairs, she told a friend to go find the sailor and deliver the message that she would indeed be going with him.

At dawn she made her way to the dock to meet the sailor and saw that the boat was gone. She ran to an old man standing at the dock and said, "I have come to meet the boat here and I sent a message for the captain of the boat last night."

The old man replied, "I have been here throughout the night, ma'am. There was no message delivered."

Couriers

This story is our story, and we have a small but crucial role in it. We are the friends who have been entrusted to deliver the message. We are not the message, God's love is. We are not even one of the main characters in God's story. God and the people we come in contact with are the main characters. Our job is to simply deliver the message of God's love. One way to look at ourselves is to realize that we possess the power to destroy a perfect love story. We carry a lot of responsibility. While we cannot claim to be the hero, the part we play is of incredible importance and actually makes the difference between a happy ending and a tragic ending.

We can change the outcome of people's lives and do great things. God will decide how effective we are, what our individual message is and whom our message is for; we just have to deliver the message. We should be willing to sail after the ship to make sure there is a happy ending, doing, as St. Peter stated, whatever needs to be done to deliver God's message of love and service.

A teacher and friend of mine named Andy was being inducted into his alma mater's Hall of Fame because of his outstanding athletic and coaching contributions to the school. He asked another friend, Kevin, to introduce him for the occasion and I remarked to Kevin what an honor it was to be Andy's presenter. Kevin replied that it was important for him not to get emotional and never say "I" in his introductory remarks.

When I asked Kevin why, he responded that at the end of his speech he didn't want anyone to know anything about him; he wanted them to know more about Andy because it was Andy who was being inducted into the Hall of Fame, not Kevin. He wanted to reflect Andy's accomplishments as if he were a mirror, not deflect attention away from Andy and direct any attention toward himself.

Like a stagehand hiding behind the curtain during a great performance, Kevin was aware of exactly what his job was and why he was doing it. His summary was a reminder of our job. In a courtroom, the word *witness* has a twofold meaning: one who has seen an event take place, and one who is willing to testify to the truth of what was seen. If we have experienced God in our lives, we must be willing to testify by our lives through our actions. That is our job: to bring God into this world through our actions.

We are entrusted with spreading God's message of love and salvation. The performance is about God; God is the star of the show and we are presenters. We are not God because we cannot provide salvation, but we are God-like because we can introduce God's love and create God's kingdom.

CHAPTER TWENTY

Playing God

At one time or another all of us even get to play the part of God. We can affect someone and be a force for good in that person's life by sharing God's love and be the picture of God someone sees today. The plans for the kingdom have been drawn up. God needs us to do the actual work, and therefore we are the laborers. During the Civil War when Abraham Lincoln was told that another general wished to assist him. Lincoln replied, "I have enough generals, I need more soldiers." We are God's soldiers, God's workers.

Mike, nearing the end of his college career, was staying at a Catholic rectory and seriously questioning what he would do after graduation. He went in to talk to the pastor, Father Bandiera, and he explained that he was confused about what he was going to do with his life. Mike knew that with his background in Agriculture he might be able to do some good in the Peace Corps, teaching people in other countries how to grow their own food, but he just wasn't sure if that's what God wanted him to do.

Mike was also aware of Covenant House in New York City, where people literally took runaway kids off the streets, away from drug dealers, pimps, and prostitution, but he didn't know if he was capable of doing that, either. Both jobs were noble, but he didn't know if he could actually be that selfless. Nevertheless, if those jobs were what God wanted him to do, he would do them to make God happy.

Father told Mike that first of all, God didn't want him to make the most painful choice. God didn't want him to be sad. God only wanted to be included in his life. Father also reminded him that it wasn't necessarily accurate to say that certain jobs are more noble than others, just different, and the people in New York were no more or less important than the people served by the Peace Corps or the children at Fairmont Catholic grade school where they were.

Hearing Father say that took a burden off Mike. He had been so worried about letting God down and doing the right job for God that he was undergoing a lot of unnecessary stress. Father reminded him that God was easy to please. As St. Francis said, "Love, and do what you will." The right thing was to act in the best interests of the people he interacted with and allow God to be a part of his life. Mike's concern about pleasing God is answered in a quote by Nikita Ivanovich Panin who wrote: "Two men please God-who serves him with all his heart because he knows him, and who seeks him with all his heart because he knows him not." Maybe where or what we do is not as important as how we show God's concern, consideration, and compassion while we do our work.

Remember that episode of M*A*S*H mentioned earlier about a bomber pilot who was shot down and thought he was Christ? Chaplain Father Mulkahey was brought in and asked the man several questions. Father said, "If you're Christ the Lord, what are you doing in an army hospital in Korea?" The pilot replied, "I'm the Lord. Where *should* I be?"

When I was in college, a roommate of mine was made a Eucharistic minister by Father Bandiera (meaning he would help distribute communion at mass). My roommate, Dave, told me he felt pretty honored to be chosen but at the same time he felt a little humbled because he knew how much of a sinner he was. Dave went to Father and said that because he was such a sinful person he had to decline because he simply wasn't worthy. Even as he was saying those words, he said, a little part of him hoped that Father would reassure him that he was being too modest and that he was a really great guy. Instead Father told Dave, "No, you're not worthy, but it's a job that has to be done."

So where should we be, what should we do, and who should we be doing things for to do God's will? Theodore Roosevelt said, "Do what you can, with what you have, where you are," which sounds very similar to what John the Baptist told the soldier and tax collector to do: feed the hungry, clothe the naked, and minister to the needy.

Faith is not selfish and actions show our faith. God's wisdom is shown to be true by its results.

Gandhi, a Hindu, said: "If every Christian lived life as Jesus did, the entire world would be Christian." After Jesus rose from the dead, his own disciples didn't recognize him when they saw him and spoke with him along the road. They recognized him through the breaking of the bread.

Although they spoke to one another about how their hearts burned in them when he spoke, it was through his actions that Jesus became known to them. They recognized him through what he did. They recognized him through his love, his spirit, and how it made them feel.

There is a bumper sticker which says, "I ain't got nothing against Jesus, it's his fan club I can't stand." Why would that be? Any of us who consider themselves to be representatives of Jesus and who act contrary to his teachings can be viewed as a hypocrite. According to the Bible, we will be judged by our fruit. We should show God to people by how we act, as Jesus did, regardless of how small or seemingly insignificant the interaction may seem.

It is good to feel enthusiastic about God and one's faith, but some people get too effusive about their relationship with God. They evangelize with high energy to anyone who will listen and to those who will not, sounding like a high pressure salesman selling divinity. While the feelings God gives us are hard to contain, they are also personal; we have to experience them for ourselves.

The excitement and joy God incites in our lives makes some people lose control over common sense and try to shove God at others. In the 1980's the United

States was awash with charismatic evangelists who told people to give, give, give to the ministry and who amassed great amounts of money in the name of God. Jim and Tammy Bakker are famous examples. Oral Roberts said God would "call him home" if he didn't receive $ 8 million dollars by a certain date.

It is against Jesus' words to take money for personal gain if it comes at someone else's expense. We all want to make our own choices and decisions and God allows us to make decisions for ourselves. Our job as Christians is to expose people to God's love and let them experience that love for themselves. Maybe we should put down the megaphone, take off our team uniform, roll up our sleeves, and get to work spreading God's love through our actions rather than by loud talking or coercion.

One day the Montel Williams television show featured a woman who, as a little girl, was teased a lot about her appearance and who became a stripper. One man who used to make fun of her all the time was also on the show. When she strutted out wearing a very revealing outfit to show him what she looked like, the man started quoting scripture to her about fearing the Lord. She waved him off, saying, "Don't give me that born-again crap" while the man continued quoting scripture.

It was clear that the man was judging the stripper, and instead of saying he was sorry for having teased her when she was young, he started preaching to her. Instead of admitting he had done anything wrong, he blamed *her*. He would not even consider the possibility that he had anything to do with her low self-esteem, which probably played a large role in driving her to seek positive reinforcement about how she looked by taking off her clothes for others.

The man never took any personal responsibility for what happened to the woman. He was a hypocrite, and he clearly judged the woman while acting as if he were her moral superior. He was acting as though he belonged to "The Club" and he was playing God. The man represented Christianity, and how he acted is why people stay away from organized religion in general. He spoke about God but acted contrary to Jesus' teachings.

Spirituality is not meant to deflect responsibility for actions *away* from us; it is meant to place responsibility for our actions squarely *on* us.

We need to show God's love, not talk about it. Talking about Christianity is not acting like a Christian. If individuals don't know that God is in their lives, it isn't because they haven't been told about God; it's because they haven't been shown God. We are the only ones who can bring God here to this moment. Our actions should show God more and us less; our actions are what God does through us.

If people are curious about God, they'll ask, but if we're good enough at showing God to them through our actions, they'll already know. What we need to radiate is God's love. St. John Bosco wrote, 'It is not enough that children be loved; they must know they are loved. Pope John XXIII stated, 'It would scarcely be necessary to teach doctrine if our lives would radiate enough." Mother Theresa commented that she was nothing more than a pencil in God's hands, and so are we.

Tiger Woods doesn't walk around the street wearing a Tiger Woods hat. People already know who he is. God is forced to hide behind the mask of our face, so the only way God can be recognized, like the risen Jesus to his disciples, is through our actions.

The famous French scientist Marie Curie wrote, "You cannot hope to build a better world without improving the individual. To that end, each of us must work for our own improvement and, at the same time, share a general responsibility for all humanity. Our particular duty being to aid those to whom we can be most useful." Our actions are how we make people aware of God.

The neighbor who brings us a meal when we can't cook or the volunteer who makes sandwiches for the homeless shelter is doing what Jesus taught. According to Jesus' teachings, accomplishments of substance and value (our treasure and trophy) are our charitable and service oriented acts. The Shakers believed that perfection in every task reflected God. Roman's 2:13 says, "For it is not in hearing the law that people are put right with God, but by doing what the law commands." God's law is to love.

On a faculty day of reflection for a private high school a few years ago, the question was asked about what made people feel like a community. Tom, a harsh, unyielding Agnostic who was the disciplinarian of the school (and was feared by the entire student body), said that what made him want to come to school more than anything else was the smile and the hug he got from Ginger, the grandmotherly head of the cafeteria when he went into the school's kitchen to get a cup of coffee. Ginger greeted Tom and everyone else the same way every morning. She didn't greet Tom or anyone to get recognition, she was just trying to make Tom feel good and show him God's love.

The gifts we are said to have are faith, hope, and love; and the greatest of these is love. It is also written that if we have faith we can move mountains. So, which is more important faith, or action? Religions tell us God wants us to believe, to have faith. Being part of the club is what gets us into heaven. Or does it?

Can we have one without the other, and where is love in this equation? Religions differ in how they answer the question. Islam says we are saved through our actions, Christianity claims we are saved through our faith and action, while Protestantism states we are saved by faith alone.

We have to answer the question of what is most important to us for ourselves, and how we answer will shape our lives. Our only chance to attain the Heaven we seek is through what we do on earth. Faith might be more important to organized religions, and faith is our personal reason for what we do, but Jesus seemed to be concerned with actions, especially in regards to how people treated the less fortunate. Love is the action Jesus spoke of.

Faith and action are like two legs to support us, and one without the other can cause us to lose our balance and hop around clumsily and awkwardly. The only way we can walk without injuring ourselves is to have the support of both legs. The only way our belief in God is functional is through both faith and action.

The Hindu belief in the spiritual cleansing of the Ganges River is a fundamental part of their faith. People bathe in the river and clean their clothes in it. Raw sewage is allowed to enter it, and so many dead bodies float in its waters that corpse-eating turtles were once considered as a means to clean up this hideously polluted river. During Holy Week in the Philippines, some Catholics actually have themselves nailed to a cross to show their faith and to show their willingness to endure pain with Christ. In these instances, actions based on faith are so extreme that the believers seem to have lost touch with reality.

We need to balance our faith and actions so we are not too extreme and attempt to live off grasshoppers and berries like John the Baptist did, or lose sight of common sense and forget that we live in this world too.

We need the support of both faith and action. Faith alone may be stagnant, but actions not directed by faith in God may be baseless. If a man was hired to help build a bridge, it would not matter whether he thought the bridge was a good idea or not, only that he do his best job building the bridge. Love is the quality of our work, action is our work and our faith is our justification. God wants us to build the kingdom on earth and we need the faith to allow God to guide us, the hope to believe in God's kingdom, and love for our actions to be successful.

If we do not believe in God and God's salvation we could consider ourselves humanitarians. Humanitarians are ipso facto not interested in building a relationship with God, but in helping humanity. Humanitarians can lose heart and have their faith in people shaken after they find out that the food that was donated to feed starving people in Africa has been stolen by warlords, or that relatives of deceased welfare recipients are still collecting the dead person's benefits.

Humans will never be perfect, even when we naively hope they will be. The nature of humanity and our world are imperfect, but God is different. God is perfection, and our faith in the perfection of God's love is our hope. That's why Christianity seems so out of touch with reality and society; it is.

To the secular person, Christianity is absurd because it is contrary to the capitalist, consumerist, selfish, individualist society and defies all popular notions of what measures success in this world. It opposes the trophy mentality and sets Christians in opposition to the material world by placing love of others rather than love of comfort as the most important concern.

"Any theory of government must be based on a realistic view of human nature. Utopian philosophies such as socialism or communism are based on beliefs in human perfection or human perfectibility. The biblical view that man is a sinner, capable of some civic virtue but basically self-centered and self-seeking, gravitates toward a different form of government."[33] Mother Theresa had the following poem written on the wall of her home for children in Calcutta, India:

> *People are often unreasonable, illogical, and self-centered; forgive them anyway.*
>
> *If you are kind, people may accuse you of selfish, ulterior motives; be kind anyway.*
>
> *If you are successful, you will win some false friends and some true enemies; succeed anyway.*
>
> *If you are honest and frank; people may cheat you; be honest and frank anyway.*
>
> *What you spend years building, someone could destroy overnight; build anyway.*
>
> *If you find serenity and happiness, they may be jealous; be happy anyway.*
>
> *The good you do today, people often forget tomorrow;do good anyway.*
>
> *Give the world the best you have, and it may never be enough; but give the world the best you've got anyway.*
>
> *You see, in the final analysis it is between you and God.*
>
> *It was never between you and them anyway.*

The poem justifies why our actions directed toward people based on God are the trophies of our lives. The reason we do any act, the "anyway" Mother Theresa writes about is God. Faith is our ability to allow God to work through our lives.

In the Bible, faith is compared to a mustard seed or speck of yeast. Both are tiny but can become huge. As yeast makes dough rise to become bread, faith can change us into new organisms. Our values, desires, goals, concerns and ideas of success can change as we grow through faith, like a mustard seed developing into a huge plant, and it all happens from the inside out as our concept of real wealth and accomplishment change through Christ.

CHAPTER TWENTY ONE

Civility

Our community, society, and world may not be as we would like them to be. If they aren't, our duty is to change what we don't like to make them better. In 1899 American Statesman Charles Schurz wrote about the United States, "Our country right or wrong, when right to be kept right, when wrong to be put right." We must feel just as possessive about our faith, our community, our society, and our world: when right to be kept right, when wrong to be put right. Special interest groups want the community to change for the sake of the individual. Jesus preached the opposite; that individuals change for the good of the community.

While a sense of entitlement leads some people to expect others to pick up after them, God's expectation is that we be the sanitation engineers and clean up the messes of society and our world. Being a good disciple is similar to being a good citizen. If we aren't involved in elections and don't vote, we have no right to complain and express our opinion about the government and elected politicians. The same is true with religion and society. If we don't work to affect change, we shouldn't complain about how things are. Attempts to improve society can create problems because some people who wish to take advantage of others for personal gain will resist any attempts to change society.

Civility is courtesy, respect, and consideration of other people. Dr. Scott Peck uses the word "civil" to describe our response to the wrongs that we see, and it may be quite confrontational. If our goal is the betterment of society, occasional grumpiness might equate with civility. In these instances grumpiness is not a choice but a responsibility and a function of our consciousness of what is right and what is wrong, an honest objective assessment of what is best for society. Our job for God is to change this world into the ideal kingdom of love God has outlined for us.

In his books on societal and social change, Dr. Peck writes that, "No matter how much joy may be its reward, pain is the inevitable and continual price of conscousness."[34] Dr. Peck observes that while Jesus was remarkably gentle with certain sinners and outcasts, he had a kind of authority that would openly berate the self-righteous. The hallmark of civility is not conflict-avoiding pretense and politeness but the commitment to deal with significant issues of organizational life.

Like medicine, or surgery, the truth may hurt, but in the long run it is always healing. Politeness never makes waves; civility is honest, open and challenging to unrealistic family or organizational norms. Women and men of conviction are always controversial. They realize they have an obligation to speak out against evil and confront it for the betterment of community, like Rosa Parks did.

She refused to give up her seat to a white man on a bus in the southern United States two generations ago. She was aware enough to discern injustice and strong enough to initiate change. It is civil to oppose others when one is doing so in submission to a higher power and for the good of society.

Erin Brockovich was a woman who stumbled upon a connection between a town's illnesses from contaminated water and a local industry cover-up. She took on the large business and won the largest settlement at that time of $333 million dollars for her clients. Her story became a blockbuster movie starring Julia Roberts.

In World Waiting to be Born, Dr. Scott Peck writes:

> " *Our lives have little, if any, meaning if they are not spiritual pilgrimages, and learning to grow out of narcissism is the core of the spiritual journey. There are two types of power: political power and spiritual power. Political power is the power to influence others through coercion. It is the power to hire and fire, punish, imprison, even kill.*

Spiritual power is the power to influence others through one's own being-by example, by kindness, by humor, by wisdom, and love. Its hallmark is humility.

The more spiritually powerful people become, the more aware they are that their power is a gift from God and has little, if anything, to do with their achievements. They understand that it is not their power but God's power racing through them. Political power has everything to do with control.

Spiritual power is a matter of what is within, encouraging rather than discouraging independence. The only civil reason to seek power is to lose it, to give it away. One mark, above all else, of the true servant leader is that she empowers others." [35]

According to Dr. Peck, people must give up thinking they know all the answers and empty themselves of their degrees, diplomas and the smugness conferred upon them by their academic or other honors while increasing their consciousness, because care of each other is based on knowledge. Community is not just something built once; it is something that must be constantly maintained and rebuilt again and again.

There is a lot at stake for ourselves and our society. If we do not take the strength God gives us, we cannot fight the evil we see in the world. The future of civilization depends on our actions. Historian Edmund Burke wrote in 1799, "The only thing necessary for the triumph of evil is for good men to do nothing." The US government is based on the role of representatives working in the best interests of others, *for*, not necessarily *with* people.

Caretakers of society sometimes make enemies by refusing to allow injustice to be done while being clear in their purpose. They are aware enough to notice the wrongs around them, active enough to initiate community-building change and persistent enough to confront resistance without giving up. The civil are strong enough to enact change while being focused enough on God to discern the genuine betterment of society.

The strength of our love for God is shown through our love for each other. Jesus embodied all of these character traits and challenges us to embody them, too. Ultimately our lives themselves should become our complete and continuous prayer and offering to God. We must try to establish our idea of good and bad, right and wrong, by trying to see things from the others person's perspective. We know too much to be naïve about the world, but allowing ourselves to become jaded won't help either.

Jesus constantly pleaded with us to approach God as a child would. To be as a child can mean child-like or childish. Childish means: unwise, juvenile, immature, and infantile. Child-like means: innocent, pure, candid, uncomplicated, unsophisticated, trusting, and simple. This latter meaning is what Jesus probably intended.

A child is aware and perceptive because children are not dominated and controlled by intellect and restraint as adults are. Children exude honesty, enthusiasm, eagerness, joy and innocence. Children are natural and astute, and intuitively trust their interpretations of events. They are emotional and not intellectual, feeling and not thinking as adults are. They have a pure, spiritual connection with God. They don't know psychology and don't know how to intellectualize because they are not yet developed intellectually. They are spirit first, then emotion. They are uncomplicated in their evaluation and act from feeling, not from intellect as adults do.

The Bible tells us not to judge. Why? Because we can't know the circumstances that make people act as they do so we should try not to assume the worst about people. That may be impossible, for we must judge actions. Some actions are good and some bad but since we can't know what's in another person's heart, we don't always have the proper perspective of a person's intent; that's what's so difficult about judging. We have an obligation to act to take evil out of the world and judge right from wrong, but it isn't always easy.

Approaching another person with a sharp blade is wrong and dangerous. If, however, I am a skilled surgeon with a scalpel about to make an incision that might save a person's life, that action is good. The circumstances can change an act from good to bad, so we have to be careful judging actions. We must look at the results, the "fruit" of the actions. As written in Matthews Gospel, God's wisdom *is* shown by its results. When bad things happen, we are not supposed to sit back and watch them happen.

If actions result in suffering rather than healing, they oppose life. God does not want people to feel pain, fear, or terror, and Jesus worked to take those things out of the world and prevent them.

Jesus spoke of peace and for peace we must work for justice. Justice is moral righteousness, the clear distinction between what is right and what is wrong. We want our idea of justice and we want it in our time right now but God has a different idea of justice than we do. Our idea of justice isn't even the same as other people's idea of justice.

Once when I was visiting my uncle, his neighbor's dog came over and urinated on my uncle's shrub. My uncle called out to his neighbor, "Don, your dog's killing my bush here, can you do something?" To which the neighbor replied, "Well Mitch, if it'll make you feel any better, you're welcome to come over and pee on my bushes." God's justice is to prevent evil by doing good. Religious and vigilante justice is administered from a limited and slanted subjective perspective.

Imagine the parents of two young boys who are fighting and maybe even hurting each other. Do the parents intervene or let the boys work it out? The parents can referee the fight or let the children take care of the situation themselves. If the parent fights the child's battles for him, the child will never learn to solve his own problems. What would we do? When children get hurt it isn't the parent's fault (unless of course the parents are negligent). If a parent hovers over a child and intervenes in every aspect of the child's life, the child will never learn to do anything for himself and will never be able to function on his own.

Children can't live in a bubble and parents can't protect them forever. It's not healthy for any child to have her parents make every decision for her, since this will keep the child from becoming strong and independent. A loving parent will let her children settle their own differences whenever feasible. God is a loving parent who allows us to make our own decisions hoping that we will choose wisely and make good decisions based on the moral and ethical rules God has established.

Not all negative acts are intentional; there is a difference between a mistake and a conscious act of wrongdoing. People who make mistakes usually receive our wrath and judgment because we interpret every mistake as intentional wrongs. A mistake is unintentional. People tend to forgive genuine mistakes, but because we tend to judge people before we know the facts, we usually condemn both mistakes and wrongdoings.

Some people try to excuse themselves from intentional misdeeds by calling them mistakes. "I can see now that beating my child to within an inch of her life was a mistake" or the professional athlete Lyle Alzado's comment that taking steroids was wrong in retrospect before he died of brain cancer. God's response to mistakes is mercy and understanding. The next time we decide to point the finger at someone, we should hook it up with all our other fingers and pray for them rather than rushing to judge them.

Rather than use the common saying, "Forgive and forget," we should, "Forgive and never forget." Even if we can't forgive people who committed evil like John Muhammad and Lee Malvo, the DC area snipers who have no remorse for killing over a dozen people around the Washington DC area in 2002, we can at least leave judgment of the individual to God. "Hate the sin and love the sinner" means to separate the person from the action.

Whenever anyone casts judgment on another person these days it's very common to hear the accused reply, "Let he who is without sin cast the first stone", "You're no better than me, so leave me alone", or "Who are you to judge me?" as some sort of absolution. It sounds like a little child saying, "You did it too!"

What is missing from such a response is the admission of guilt, along with our desire to not make that mistake again. Fascism and murder are not "mistakes," they are purposefully inflicted evils. When high school seniors in Northbrook, Illinois engaged in an extreme hazing incident in which senior girls kicked, punched, beat up and rubbed feces and mud over the bodies of juniors at the school, the guilty students brought parents and lawyers to their defense, asking for leniency so the seniors wouldn't miss their prom or have the incident on their record.

This shows an unfortunate lack of responsibility for their actions. These seniors didn't apologize to the victim's, either. This incident was not a "mistake," it was carefully planned. Often individuals will commit an act they know is wrong because the benefit outweighs the cost. They know they will not be punished severely even if they get caught because it is easier to get forgiveness than permission. When we commit a sin we must apologize to God. The issue is personal responsibility and misrepresentation of ourselves to God.

A church sign-board said, "Confession without repentance is just bragging." The most important part of contrition is being sorry for our sin because we know it was wrong, not because we got caught.

As we attempt to enact God's will by force and rid the world of evil, like soldiers in God's army, we must remember that God's justice may not be instantaneous. In the gospel of Matthew 13: 24–30, 37–43 we read that:

> *Jesus describes the story of a man who sowed good seed in his field, and an enemy of his came and sowed weeds in the same field. The man did not pull up the weeds for fear of killing the wheat, instead allowing both to grow up together where the harvester would separate the wheat from the weeds.*
>
> *When the disciples asked Jesus to explain what the parable meant, Jesus answered: "The man who sowed the good seed is the Son of Man; the field is the world; the good seed is the people who belong to the kingdom; the weeds are the people who belong to the Evil One; and the enemy who sowed the weeds is the devil. The harvest is the end of the age, and the harvest workers are angels.*

Just as the weeds are gathered up and burned in the fire, so the same thing will happen at the end of the age: the Son of Man will send out his angels to gather up out of his kingdom all who cause people to sin and all others who do evil things, and they will throw them into the fiery furnace, where they will cry and grind their teeth.

Then God's people will shine like the sun in their Father's kingdom. Listen, then, if you have ears!

We may get frustrated at how much evil is in the world that won't go away, but Matthew's reading can remind us that evil will always be with us and some people will always choose evil. Justice will be administered in God's time, not ours. In practical terms we can keep people safe from dangerous people wishing to cause pain and injury. We can be God's police but God is the judge, not us.

CHAPTER TWENTY TWO

Discerning versus Judgmental

In the early 1900s, St. Maria Goretti was the victim of an attempted rape by her second cousin. When she resisted him, he stabbed her to death. Italian law did not have the death penalty, so he was sentenced to life in prison, which meant 25 years. The man ended up becoming a Franciscan monk. He wrote a letter of apology to Maria Goretti's family and even attended her Canonization, the ceremony in which she was named a Saint. If he had been given the death penalty, he wouldn't have had the chance to give his life over to Christ.

As we work to prevent evil from being done, it is important for us to remember that Jesus always held out the possibility for people to change and always allowed them the opportunity to begin again. Evil can only be conquered by love and Jesus never hurt anyone. There was no retribution, stoning, payback or killing involved in his justice. Our concern should be to do what we can to prevent evil and leave judgment to God.

It is an unrealistic expectation to expect ourselves not to judge. To act with compassion and understanding, we must judge others to gain perspective and discernment. Discernment is inclusive, judgment is exclusive. Jay was a boy in junior high school who was taking physical education. His teacher constantly gave Jay a grade of D and his personal best time for running the mile was 8:55. He usually ran the mile in well over nine minutes. Since the boy was overweight and suffered from adolescent insecurity and inferiority, this grade only lowered his self-esteem and worsened his self-image.

His teacher began taking classes to improve his teaching methods and discovered that measuring pulse during exercise is a measure of how hard the body is working. The teacher discovered that there is a value called the target pulse, which is a general guide to an individual's highest possible heart rate during activity. Target pulse is calculated by subtracting 220 minus the age of the person. Since Jay was twelve years old, his target pulse was 220-12, or 208 beats per minute.

The next time the class ran the mile, the teacher had the students measure their pulse at the end of the run. When Jay's pulse was found to be over 200 beats per minute, Jay received a grade of A even though he ran the mile in 8:45. His pulse showed that he was performing at almost 100% of his ability.

Jay was originally being judged by standards that should not have been applied to him. The teacher judged him using a standard which was appropriate for him by altering his perspective and perception from judgment to discernment. He received justice when his performance was ultimately evaluated based on his effort, not the outcome alone.

Sensitivity and awareness lead to tolerance. Tolerance does not mean agreement with but acceptance. As we grow impatient for justice and want people who commit evil acts brought to justice immediately, we should remember that justice is God's to deliver. What we can do is model Christian behavior. Jesus showed kindness, tolerance, and patience.

God has opted to allow us to choose to belong to God or to the Devil. In the book *World Waiting to be Born* Dr. Peck writes "God gave Satan free will and cannot destroy, only create. God does not punish. To create us in his own image, God gave us free will. To have done otherwise would have been to make us puppets or hollow mannequins. Yet to give us free will God had to forswear the use of force against us. The Christian God is a God of restraint. Having forsworn the use of power against us, if we refuse his help, he has no recourse but, weeping, to watch us punish ourselves."[36] When we see evil we should not say how could *God* let this happen, but how can *we* allow this to happen?

Stewardship

We are all "stewards" of God's kingdom, God's vision of shared concern for one another. A steward is a person who manages another's property or finances. A partner has to answer to someone else, where a sole owner answers only to himself. We have to answer to God ourselves. We must actively work to manage that kingdom, this world and this life wherever we are by loving as completely as Jesus did.

Near the end of 7:30 A.M. mass one Sunday at Saint Thomas Moore Catholic Church in Chapel Hill North Carolina, the priest introduced a woman called Helen to speak on behalf of the stewardship program at the parish. The stewardship program is an attempt to get parishioners more involved in running the church's many organizations, groups, and programs. The appeal is for parishioners to take ownership and more actively assume an operational role of parish activities. When Father told the congregation to sit down and listen to the woman, there was a slight groan, as if everyone was thinking only about how this talk would delay the conclusion of mass another five or ten minutes.

Helen spoke of her own struggles with her faith. She said she had been away from the church for years but had never stopped going to church altogether. Then one week her priest spoke of how, when we reach heaven, we will be required to give an account of our lives to the people to the right of us and the people to the left of us.

Helen spoke of being so affected by that statement that she decided right then and there to get more involved in some activities around the parish. Over the course of months and years, she found herself doing more and more. She started a prayer group, a service program, and she volunteered at the grade school. She also began feeling better and better about herself and her life. She said, "These are not things I do but things that God does through me. God will not be outdone in generosity. As much as I have given, God has always given me more." When she finished speaking, the congregation applauded and had a clearer sense of their role in the church.

Our attitude of stewardship should extend beyond our church, and our church should be a source of service to the community. The people we come in contact with must be under our care, our stewardship. Our stewardship must also extend to the society we inhabit.

We and God are partners

As partners with God, we take on the responsibility for making sure God's work gets done. During the 2000 United States Presidential elections, Howard Stern, a nationally syndicated shock-jock, was talking on his radio show about the candidates. When someone mentioned that George Bush was a born-again Christian, Stern responded by saying, "Oh, I don't even want to hear about that crap, that Santa Claus stuff." Stern's comparison of Christ to Santa Claus was intended to mock belief in Christ, but upon further review, Stern may be closer to the truth than he thought. Although Santa is a legend, and Jesus Christ was both God and human being, they both share many similarities. Christ *is* similar to Santa because they both bring us gifts.

Santa brings toys and other presents; Christ brings forgiveness for our sins, the Holy Spirit and salvation. They both want people to be happy. Both know when we've been naughty or nice (but only Santa puts coal in our stocking if we've been bad) and both bring about a sense of wonder and awe, especially in children.

The film *Miracle on 34th Street* tells the story of how Santa Claus was shown in a court of law to be real, not just because of the belief of a little girl but through the hard evidence of bags of letters addressed to "Santa" presented in court. The movie didn't actually prove the existence of Santa Claus, just as we can't prove the existence of God to someone who doesn't want to believe. But it does illustrate how the evidence of God to ourselves is based on what we feel and the proof of God to others is shown through our actions.

Ted Turner called Christianity "a Religion of losers" in a 1989 interview with the Dallas Morning News. Mr. Turner spoke of how his sister died a slow and painful death from lupus even though he had prayed for her for an hour every day. The imperfections of religious people and religious organizations were also brought up to show how God is of no consequence to this life.

He also spoke about the hypocrisy and intolerance of Christianity and religion. This statement seems to suggest distrust or anger against Christians and all institutional religion. Maybe people have so much hostility toward God because of their fear of the unknown. Certainly Jesus did not have any trophies and is not in any Hall of Fame. He lived simply, owned nothing and lost his life in a very disrespectful manner, but we have a light at the end of this life's tunnel because Jesus Christ brought salvation to all of us.

Money can't buy us salvation and we can't take our possessions with us. There is no first-class section in heaven. Maybe that is what brings about feelings of resentment or hate in wealthy and famous people like Mr. Stern and Mr. Turner. They view God as outdated, pre-scientific, mythological baggage. Money, status and influence can buy many things. Maybe these men won't allow themselves to need or want God because they keep trying to buy God and the joy of life, but God isn't for sale. God is free in the same quantity and quality to the penniless beggar as to the multi-millionaire or famous radio personality.

Comedian George Carlin once remarked about, "People who believe that fairy tale, that superstition about some man in the sky" and how bad it was to make people feel guilty. If we want to be guilt-free, we have to ignore our ideas of right and wrong. The if-it-feels-good-do-it days of the 1960's and 1970's were attempts to live without a conscience and be self-absorbed and self-centered. Casual sex, drugs, and alcohol indulgence were attempts to feel good which many people ultimately found unsatisfying because they were temporary "highs".

That experiment in self-pleasuring left a lot of people unfulfilled and ultimately seeking something more. People need ethics because we need to know there are consequences to our actions. "If there is no God, no heaven, no hell," says Professor Jerry L. Walls of Asbury Theological Seminary writing in <u>Christianity Today</u>, "there simply is no persuasive reason to be moral."

Christianity is not something we should try to intellectualize; it is felt in our hearts. God is not like a math problem with one definite answer. God is all of the answers, refusing to be defined in the empirical terms that intellectuals and nonbelievers attempt to use, but simply felt in love. When people attempt to disprove the existence of God and make references to "that Santa Claus stuff, that crap" or call believers "losers," their predisposed, "you're wrong" attitude is an attempt to tell believers what we feel. It is a sad reality that these nay-sayers have made the choice *not* to feel God's love and disapprove of our choice to do so.

Remember the story of the Little Red Hen? She asked various animals to help her bake bread but all refused her. They did not trust her to actually follow through on her word. When she baked the bread, all the animals wished to eat it, but then it was too late. They had already positioned themselves as not believing in the bread as a possible reality.

Nay-sayers refuse to help and even actively attack those who work to spread God's message.

Unfortunately, they may have to face the truth and they will be forced to eat their words. The one difference is God will always allow the truly penitent to change.

Individuals and institutions attack believers with open distain, claiming belief in God is a crutch or weakness. By trying to intellectualize our existence and prove that God doesn't exist, these individuals prove their own point, that God can't be explained any more than we can tell a blind person what the color blue looks like.

Bumble Bee's are too heavy to fly, yet they do. No one knows why, except God. This phenomenon has been studied extensively, with no scientific answer. People who claim something must be proven to be true assume that nothing exists without proof. The problem for these individuals is not everything can be proven, and a math equation even exists stating that not all things can even be proven.

We can relate our belief in God through the way it makes us feel much the same way we can relate the warmth of blue or the brightness of yellow through what the colors make us feel. The incredible genius behind God's plan of salvation is that it is freely given and actively chosen by us, while the only proof of God is in that which cannot be seen but only felt: love.

We cannot prove the existence of God to those who will not believe, we can simply show God's love. We cannot see glass, but it certainly exists, and can be literally felt if we attempt to go through it. Glass is similar to our faith; it is what we *see* our life *through*.

We are partners working on God's behalf toward the same goal. God needs us to build the kingdom. We represent God and must be concerned with what God would do. The slogan "WWJD," or "What would Jesus do?" reminds us to keep focused on doing God's work through our every action. Professional golfer Payne Stewart, who died tragically in a plane crash several years ago, wore a WWJD bracelet on his wrist to remind him of his responsibility to Jesus, and many other people do the same.

We have a moral, ethical, and personal responsibility to the partnership between ourselves and God. Our actions either create or fail to create God's kingdom *here*. We must shoulder the responsibility personally and adopt the saying about God's kingdom: *If it is to be, it is up to me*.

The attempted removal of God from society, especially in the United States, is evidenced by the slow but subtle changes in our traditions. The United States was founded as a place where individuals could worship God without persecution, a right that is protected in the Constitution.

In American public schools, Christmas has been replaced by "Winter Holiday" and Easter break by "Spring Break" in public schools. "Silent Night" has been replaced with "Sleigh Ride" and "Winter Wonderland." Prayer has either been removed or altogether replaced by a moment of silence. Christmas, the observance of Christ's birth is even referred to as Xmas by those wishing to remove Christ from the observance. The effect of all this is the separation of God from society and from public view.

Individuals claim to be offended by Christian traditions such as the Christmas and Easter holidays, but Christians should be offended by these recent developments and attempted restrictions of their right to worship. In 2003 a Washington DC area radio station sponsored a "Nondenominational Christmas concert." How can the recognition of Christ's birth be without religious definition? Some retail stores have even stopped referring to Christmas and instead refer to the Happy Holidays.

While some individuals and groups attempt to take away our right to believe in God and attempt to exclude religion and God from society, we have an obligation to defend that right for everyone. There is no state mandated religion in the United States. Belief in God is not required and remains an option, but the alarming secularization of American society requires our action and intervention.

Supreme Court Justice Anthony Scalia spoke at a high school father-son dinner in 2003 and stated that, "In 1947 the Supreme Court ruled, 'We in the United States are a religious people and certain religious customs are an inherent part of our American culture. A decade later, the Court began to act in a neutral way, not only among all religions, but even towards religion and nonreligious views.'"[37]

The change has continued to intensify the public pressure to remove any and all references to God from public view. As partners with God, our job as Christians is our personal responsibility, our obligation to work for God's inclusion in society. In 2003 the Ten Commandments were ordered removed from a courthouse in Georgia because of the supposed separation of church and state. When Chief justice Roy Moore defied the law, he was removed from office.

The drafting of a European Union Constitution in 2003 makes no mention of God at all. The Bible mentions that if we deny God, God could deny us. As partners, we must stick up for God as we would defend a family member. According to an email making its way around the Internet, a child wrote and asked why God wasn't at Columbine High School or at other public schools when similar tragedies occurred. The reply came from God, "I'm not allowed in public schools."

Jesus was a teacher. God's classroom is our world. Consider how different people respond to God. As a teacher, God is sometimes seen as unfair because we see people who cheat and don't get caught do well, but the one time we don't do our homework we get caught. Some see God as a little lacking as a disciplinarian by allowing evil and pain to be inflicted, allowing people to make decisions for themselves, by not always telling people what to do, allowing people to be independent and figure out for themselves; and lenient by allowing people to start over and retake tests.

God doesn't enforce the rules concerning chewing gum or skirt length, and pays as much attention to the dorky and weird students as the cool people and the jocks. God doesn't care about being liked but seems concerned only that the students know he loves them.

God's class is based on our freedom, on choices and decisions to pay attention to the activities of our lives. We students are made responsible for every action, graded on our effort as we take notes, our behavior, and involvement. We have all the power to retake, do over, and be forgiven. Our class is black and white, we decide by our actions, our choices what grade, what trophy we receive.

Many students in school receive information for 45 minutes, passively sitting in fear because the teacher has complete control of the class, not being able to breathe loud, but without any active learning going on. Some resent and hate it, make excuses, never take advantage of the opportunities, while some feel empowered and excel.

Our lives are our class. We choose what we get out of them by how we respond. After establishing the set up-the class has little to do with teacher, but everything to do with us as students and how we respond. It is not exactly as we want it to be, but we have to create what we want, to make class and the classroom environment as we desire. We have the obligation to work to make our lives and world as we would like them to be and allow God to enter it through our actions.

CHAPTER TWENTY THREE

Building community

We are all position players, like the members of a baseball team. We all have different abilities, gifts, and jobs. We have many opportunities to "play ball," to make a difference, to inspire others and spread God's love. Without a team, a player is still a player, but he is not actively performing. The players are cheated when they aren't given the opportunity to play. Some players simply stop playing altogether. Religions should provide the means for the faithful to work at the soup-kitchen, volunteer at homeless shelters, and sponsor food and clothing drives to help the less fortunate. Remember, religion and churches can be the ties that bind community members together just as shoe laces bring a shoe together. Religion comes from *religio*: to connect.

However, it's not healthy for us to *need* the church to get closer to God. In any relationship, it's not healthy for us to need another person to make us complete. In the same way, it's not good for us to depend on the church blindly throughout our spiritual journey. Questioning, having disagreements and problems with our church should not drive away all church-going people to worship on their own.

On the contrary, it should drive people to church because religion should be the opportunity to bring God to us. We should *want* to be a part of the church, just like a player wants to play for a team. The church is the uniform of our faith, but we can still play without a uniform. Playing, after all, is what's important.

If we can't count on the Church, then why join the church? The answer is because when we unite, we form the church Jesus intended when he said, "When two or more are gathered in my name, I am there." The church may act as if it "chooses us," with all the rites of initiation and sacramental obligations imposed on believers. The institution may appear to hold all the power over us, but the power is all ours. We choose to be the church. A personal partnership with God should lead us to church because we want to go to be connected. The church should be filled with spiritual, aware individuals freely acting as a community as Jesus defined it.

If members of the church hierarchy seem to be concerned more with looking toward their own retirement or protecting the interests of the institutional church than guiding and protecting their church members, we need to correct the problem by being Consumer Advocates for God. The potential of the church as an opportunity to work toward a common goal is in our hands.

Margaret Schettler was 22 years old and in love with the Catholic Church's ministry to the poor when she found out that a pedophile priest was visiting at the parish she volunteered at and confronted the church to admit it. When the church ignored and mislead her, she became disillusioned. Today, Schettler still works as a lay minister, teaching adult confirmation classes and planning special Masses at Our Lady of Grace Church in Encino, California. She is working for her God, attempting to keep right the things that are right, and make right the things that are wrong with the church.

Possibly the clearest example of how people working together can accomplish much more than they could accomplish individually is the Amish barn-raising. If a member of the Amish community is constructing a new barn, or loses a barn to fire or wind, the entire Amish community of men, women, and children come together to help construct a barn for their "brethren."

Religions *can* be the tie to bind us all together, but religion can often cause schisms. The terror of 9 / 11, caused by fanatics who claimed to be avenging God, has deepened the rift between Christians and the Arab world. The absurdity of the term "Holy war" and the supposed carrying out of Gods will through death and destruction should encourage us to find a more civil means to solve this global and regional animosity. Our connection to each other will be completed, not through colonial expansion of any faith, or by violence, but by greater under-standing and service to each other and attempts to find common ground. We and God need each other. God needs workers and we need God's kingdom to be established.

Many people, when asked why they don't go to church, expose their trophy case mentality and reply, "I don't get anything out of it." If going to church is drudgery, we won't be paying attention, so how *can* we get anything out of it? Church isn't a place where we get anything; it's a place where we give. Church is our opportunity to change from the *take* mode to the *give* mode and connect with God and community.

Belonging to a church does not mean having blind faith or totally agreeing with everything espoused there. Being a church member is like being a family member. Being part of a family does not mean that we support every action of other family members or that we agree with everything they do. We argue and fight with members of our family, but that doesn't mean we cease being a member of the family. We can't stop being connected.

Jesus spoke of bringing people together, not putting up barriers and separating a community. People who claim that they don't need to go to church because they can talk to God from where they are seek to justify making their association with God convenient for them. Faith has little to do with our personal convenience; Christianity is based on being of service to others.

We are either an isolated, detached group of individuals or a community of believers. We are connected to God and each other. The Presbyterian

Church sponsors trips to Mexico to build houses; the Baptist Church runs a soup-kitchen from its property, and the missionary group of Brothers and Priests takes young volunteers to Appalachia to build houses.

Each of these groups does God's work, although it's certainly not convenient for them. Our religious activities must have a social conscience and we must return our institutions' concern back to community service. Collecting coats, blankets, and making sandwiches is creating God's kingdom. It is not the function of society to serve institutions; religious institutions exist to serve the community through their actions.

A particularly meaningful article on the value of religion was written by Gary Eisler in Mensa Magazine in 2001. As someone who didn't like all the packaging of religion and who thought of himself as more spiritual than religious, Eisler wrote about how he was influenced by acts of kindness from people of many faiths in different circumstances during his life. He wrote:

> *"Spirituality morphs into religion in the cauldron of life. That's because religions-many of them-are the vehicle through which certain spirits enter the world. The Presbyterians, with whom I affiliate in Portland, Oregon, are the dearest, kindest, most caring people you could ask for. I don't know how I would have gotten through my wife's illness, let alone my own, without their personal care, support, and prayers. There were times, for*

example, when my wife's breast cancer had so devastated her that I was on constant duty to change her morphine pump, clean her open wounds and bathe her. Those were the times my care group from church brought me meals, cleaned my house-one of them even washed my wife's feet.

A couple years later when I was going in for chemotherapy week after week, it was someone from my church who drove me there and was also there for support many of the times when the doctor gave me bad news. And my brother, an Orthodox Jew, took time off from work and came across the country to be with me before a stem-cell transplant. He saw his kid brother bald, gaunt, and sallow from months of an unsuccessful struggle to abate my non-Hodgkin's lymphoma. Somehow the guy was able to kid me the way he did when we were children-he helped me laugh again even when I was sick and afraid.

Similarly, the hospital where I was sequestered for three weeks was run by an order of Catholic nuns, and the people who cared for me did so as if it were more of a mission than a job. Despite all the years of dealing with illness, I have not fallen into financial ruin, thanks to the financial generosity of my clients-especially a businessman / ordained minister of a nondenominational church who continued to pay me even when I was unable to work.

I wish I would say, "Religion-who needs it? We ought to be able to face the mysteries of existence without having to see them through someone else's paradigm. I want nothing to do with any organization whose teachings have been the impetus for wars, torture, and extortion. Everything is ultimately understandable and I can take care of myself, thank you."

But I can't. It may be a short leash I'm on, but at least I'm still here, and I must credit the spirit working through organized religions for that.

Most religions teach that there are two spirits aloft in this world: one is cruel, stultifying, and greedy. The other is life sustaining, loving and caring. Few of us are so unrealistic as to believe that both spirits are not at work everywhere-even within religions themselves.

I guess it's just like being in love. The object of your affection probably has some faults. There may even be those who wonder what in the world you see in the other person. But you don't dwell on the negative because you see your sweetie through the eyes of love. Maybe that's why proud people are humbled... so that their need can force them to see the good that religion has to offer.[38]

This passage points out that although religions and its members are imperfect, community assistance is the work of God and the creation of God's kingdom.

Religion creates Gods church: community. St. Francis de Sales said, "The test of a preacher is that his congregation goes away saying, not 'What a lovely sermon' but 'I will do something.'" Religion is the means of mobilizing the community to service. Religion is not perfect but is the team we play for. Hopefully every religion is playing God's game of loving our neighbor and the team playing the "best" is the one where God's love is found the most abundantly.

In Community

When Jesus rose from the dead and appeared to the disciples, Thomas was not among them and he would not believe anyone who told him that Jesus had actually appeared. Later, when Thomas was with the others, Jesus appeared again and Thomas believed what he saw for himself. When Thomas was by himself and isolated from the community he doubted Jesus' divinity, but when he was with his community, he believed. He believed because he experienced the event for himself. We can remove our doubts and disbelief by our association with other people; our community is our connection to each other.

The largest living thing in the world, the giant redwood tree, cannot survive on its own. It has such shallow roots that it will topple over if left to grow in isolation. When it grows among other redwoods its roots intertwine with those of the other trees, giving it such tremendous strength that it can withstand even high winds. Like the redwood, we expose our weaknesses and imperfections in isolation, but gain strength in community.

We are told that, through religions, we are taken to God and Heaven and we are simply passengers or spectators in our own lives. But maybe we are not just passengers on a big train going to heaven and maybe religion is not the ticket booth and God is not our engineer or driver, after all.

God is here to show us how to obtain the trophy we desire, but through our decisions God lets us drive our own car to Heaven. We want to get to Heaven but we aren't sure how to get there and we can't get there on our own because only God can see the map. Although we don't get to see the map, we get our directions from God. Our relationship with God gives us our direction.

It is up to us to separate our relationship with God from our relationship with people or institutions. Institutions are operated by imperfect people and therefore are always positioned to let us down. Our faith in people will constantly be shaken because human beings are imperfect.

If we are looking for assistance to find God, religion can do that for us, but God must end up inside of us, not in the church building. God is the only perfection. God will never let us down, and we should never allow anyone or anything to shake our faith in God. Our relationship with the church will not bring us salvation; our relationship with God will bring us eternal life. Religion is a journey of the heart to God. Religion is not spirituality, but a conduit to the spiritual and the sacred. Religion is a means to serve.

Some see the unending turmoil in organized religion as a reason to distance themselves from God, which is the greatest tragedy. Many individuals have stopped going to church because of the actions of one minister or priest, or have abandoned a religion because of a disagreement or dissatisfaction with one clergy member. For example, when a priest refused to allow one Catholic couple to get married in the church because they had no involvement with the parish, the couple reacted in anger, completely disassociated themselves from the religion, and cut off their association with the church altogether.

We can leave organized religion and criticize it, or we can initiate change by contacting our religious leaders to make sure that church hierarchy responds to our concerns. Church officials represent us the same way elected political officials represent their constituencies. Voice of the Faithful, a group founded by Catholic laypersons in Massachusetts, is petitioning the Pope to give lay members of the church more power and say in the operation of the church. This group seeks to actively involve lay Catholics in the governance and guidance of the church.

If we believe that priests should marry, women should be allowed to be ordained as priests, congregations should have a say in the appointment and assignment of priests and ministers, then we have an obligation to be heard and our strength comes from our unity. If we believe the congregation should have a more active role in how contributions to the church are spent, we must work for that to happen. Although congregations donate the money for the church's needs, the institutional church owns every building and asset in every religion. Jesus' emphasis was on the communal, not the institutional church.

When institutions get too big they can lose sight of the individual member to protect the institution. Consider those who lost their retirement savings in the Enron corporation collapse. Corrupt high-ranking officials illegally cashed in millions of dollars of stock while the retirement stock of the employees was becoming devalued.

We say we're having "one of those days" when one person or several people do something to make us sad or mad for our entire day, but no person or institution should affect our relationship with God by moving us farther away from God. Finding fault with organized religion, some people, like the couple above, will simply leave God out of their lives altogether. One course of action is to abandon ship and form our own religion, as Martin Luther and the Protestant Reformation churches did hundreds of years ago when they broke away from the Catholic Church.

Churches and institutions can also act in the best interest of the institution and protect themselves rather than their members. Intolerance and scandal is a historical part of every religion. The Protestant Reformation was a reaction to Papal power. The splintering of the Protestant church into many different denominations came about from the failure of those formed churches to agree on how to run their organization. We can't always count on the church to act in our best interest, but God does everything in our spiritual best interest. God's primary interest is our eternal life and our salvation.

We cannot allow our relationship with God to be hurt by the constant crises of our times, or allow individuals in the church to separate us from each other when we become aware that a priest or minister is also an adulterer or pedophile. In 2003 the Catholic Bishop of Phoenix struck a man with his car, killing him, and left the scene of the crime. God and the Catholic Church didn't commit any crime, the Bishop did. Just as we should separate the person from the action, we should separate God from the church. We must see the incident as a lack of character in the Bishop, not the imperfection of God.

Why Me?

As much as God attempts to contact us through people and circumstances in our daily existence, sometimes God may be trying to get our attention in ways we interpret as negative. We may blame God and question why things happen but sometimes misfortune, by our reaction to it, can benefit us or others.

A man stranded on a desert island prayed and prayed for God to save him. He built a crude shelter for himself and one day, as he was out trying to gather some food, he saw some smoke. He ran back and found his shelter in flames. He immediately began screaming at God about how God had failed to come through for him until he noticed a plane approaching. The pilot of the plane said that if he hadn't seen the smoke, he never would have stopped at the island.

A victim of a horrific flood scrambled to the top of his house as the water rose. A neighbor passed by in a raft and offered his assistance to the man but the man said no, God would take care of him. Sometime later a boat came by and again the man declined assistance, saying God would take care of him. Much later, as the water level rose, only the very top of the man's house was exposed above the water. A helicopter appeared and offered to take the man aboard but the man declined, saying God would take care of him.

The man died and in heaven he confronted the Lord. "I had faith in you. You said you would take care of me but you didn't."

God replied, "I sent you a raft, a boat, and a helicopter. What more could I do for you?"

We may not see the reason why God sometimes says "No" to us. Children often resent parents and other adults for setting limits, disciplining them for misbehavior and denying them their whims by not allowing them to go out without cleaning their room or not letting them stay out past 11:00 P.M.. The children might not like those experiences at the time but later may realize that the discipline was for their own benefit. We, like children, need to show a little more faith that God knows what is in our best interest while we may not.

How could God allow this to happen?

When two troubled students at Columbine High School in Colorado brutally murdered fellow students and a teacher in April 1999, the Bishop of Denver responded to two questions citizens in the area asked. The first question was "How could God allow something like this to happen?" The second question was "Why us?"

The Bishop was asked why God had chosen to afflict that particular community. When tragedy struck them, they asked, "Why us?" The Bishop responded, "Why not us?" Why should we be spared life's pain? The Apostles of Jesus and many disciples met with a tragic death, and Jesus himself was brutally put to death, so our desire to escape from pain might be wishful thinking. God may not keep us from physical pain but God rescues us from emotional pain.

God knows all about pain and suffering. God knows the pain of losing a child, having sent Jesus down to earth with a message of love and service only to see that son put to death as a criminal. We forget that God went through every emotion we can go through when tragedy strikes us, and God might feel as depressed, shocked, angry, and sad as we do. God experienced this suffering to save humanity from sinfulness.

God promises us salvation in heaven, not earthly riches or a pain-free life. Salvation does not apply to physical death but to spiritual death. One Sunday, during his sermon, Father Bart Smith remarked about the tragedy of death and stated, "Death is not the worst thing that could happen; the worst thing that could happen is for us to lose our salvation."

God does not want bad things to happen and God doesn't make this world perfect, only we can do that.

God hates evil but God provided mankind with the gift of free will. As a result one may decide to follow good or evil. God does not restrict our ability to make our own decisions.

In Montgomery County Maryland in 2000, a Catholic priest, Father Thomas Wells, was murdered in his rectory. His parishioners could not believe how such a senseless act could occur. As people searched for reasons, many of Father Wells' parishioners recalled how he loved being a priest and how he tried to show how we should live every day as if it were our last. He preached that there was too much uncertainty in the world to live any other way. We have to confront the possibility that today might be all we have, and give our attention to every moment.

There is nothing good about the terrorist attack of September 11 2001, or the countless other times throughout the course of history when murder, genocide, and evil were perpetrated on others. However, those events do change history. Before the attacks of 9/ 11, few if any Americans believed that it was possible that hate and anger against America would be substantial enough to lead anyone to willingly cause death and destruction, or that people would actually kill themselves just to inflict such devastation.

Present day America is watchful of terror and the entire world is on edge, warily watching for hostility and evil. Because complacency can diminish our awareness, complacency is also an enemy of ours. Suffering tests the strength of our will. *In World Waiting to Be Born*, Dr. Scott Peck writes: "I believe a strong will is the greatest blessing that can be bestowed on a person-not because it guarantees success, but because a weak will guarantees failure."[39]

CHAPTER TWENTY FOUR

Meek does not mean timid

If we model ourselves after Jesus of Nazareth, we should look at how he handled himself when he was on trial in front of Pilot and Herod, about to be put to death. When he was brought in front of these powerful men, he might have been able to save his own life if he had compromised his position or if he had tempered what he said and backed off just a little bit. As he was confronted with the reality of his own death, he uttered the words, "Not my will, but yours be done."

Jesus understood that submitting to Gods will would benefit all of mankind and thus allowed himself to be the sacrifice to save all of us. During crises in our lives we can claim God has abandoned us and disassociate ourselves from God or we can rationalize compromising our beliefs to spare ourselves pain and claim we are compromising for the greater good, but we probably don't have the fate

293

of all humanity dependent on our decision. Are we backing off our beliefs for God's good, or our own? Jesus showed the strength to hold fast to his belief in God's plan, even when it meant his own death. Can we do the same? Do we show the strength to follow our convictions, even if it might cause us personal harm?

Joan of Arc lived in the early 1400's in France. She heard "Voices" or what she referred to as her counsel who she recognized as St. Michael, St. Margaret, and St. Catherine. The voices came to her and guided her to make herself known to a commander of Charles VII and later to the ruler himself. After defeating the English and sending them from Orleans, she was abandoned by the French rulers, the Catholic Church, and taken prisoner by the English.

Joan was tried for Heresy against the church and burned at the stake, as those around her attempted to prove her to be a witch. Until the last she called out to Jesus and held strong to her convictions while all institutions and individuals around her compromised theirs. Only after the Church authorities revisited the circumstances surrounding her trial and death hundreds of years after she was murdered was Joan made Saint Joan.

Being timid means being afraid, cowering, and being afraid might even keep us from acting. We must act even if we are afraid. Fear cannot paralyze us to inaction. When we are weak God provides our strength and that allows the credit for what we accomplish to be God's even though we love for other people to know what we've done. We love the popularity but

God deserves the credit. Meek does not mean timid. Meek means gentle, submissive and compliant to God knowing God is the source of our strength.

The strength of our will is exhibited in how we respond to adversity. A little boy named Adam Walsh was abducted from a shopping mall years ago and murdered. His father John established the television program "America's Most Wanted" and, since its inception, this television show has been responsible for the capture of over eight hundred of the most wanted criminals in the United States. A wealthy man's son died and the heart-broken father became listless and saw no reason for continuing to live. His son came to him in a dream and told his father to care for other people's children, leading that man to establish Stanford University.

As the Passion of Jesus is read on Palm Sunday during Lent, recounting Jesus' triumphant entrance into Jerusalem, trial and crucifixion, some individuals complain that during the service the faithful should not be the ones reading the part of the crowd crucifying Jesus. After all, we are the good guys who are in church, trying to do God's will; we weren't there when the masses crucified Jesus.

We weren't there during Hitler's reign of terror when millions of Jews were murdered, during the times throughout history when occupied peoples became slaves to their conquerors, during the times of slavery in the United States or when European settlers of the United States virtually erased the civilization of the American Indian. So why should we be put in the position of being the crowd that crucified Jesus? Because we are still in that position.

Evil is with us today in the horror of individuals such as Gary Ridgeway, the Green River killer in Seattle, Washington who murdered dozens of women in the 1980's and we must always be watchful. An 11-year-old Florida girl, Carlie Bruscia, was kidnapped and murdered in February 2004 and her abduction was caught on a surveillance tape. We must always put ourselves in the situations here awful things happened and not only ask ourselves what we *would* do, but what *are* we doing about the injustices around us now.

The disciples and followers of the Lord ran away when Jesus was crucified because they feared for their lives. Would we have acted any differently? In Jesus' time people faced severe oppression and crisis and both are still with us today. Each generation faces troubled times and critical situations and today is no different than thousands of years ago.

Instead of saying "Why me?" we should be saying, "Because!" Instead of passively watching the circumstances of our life, we should be taking it upon ourselves to act to improve the moral and ethical direction of our world and society. In Chicago, single mothers Desiree Smith, Vanessa Lazar, and Ericka Smith have taken it upon themselves to raise money to help feed Famine victims with Save the Children.

Even if it is impossible for us to "forgive" evil individuals, it is critical for us to acknowledge the evil and try to prevent it from being repeated. If we don't acknowledge the holocaust, slavery, and the existence of sexual predators, how do we protect the world and prevent evil? Just as we remember fascism and ethnic cleansing throughout time we can be watchful to never allow child abuse or cereal killings to happen again.

When Moses came down from forty days on a mountain to find approximately three thousand people dancing around a golden idol in the shape of a calf, he chastised the people and reminded them that nothing was to be worshipped in the same way as God. As a result of this action by a few, the nation of about three million Jews was punished to illustrate, according to Rabbi Ken Spiro, God's expectation that knowledge makes us responsible for our actions and accountable for ourselves and others. The Rabbi states that Judaism teaches that if we are not part of the solution, we are part of the problem.

A modern example of inactivity is the reaction and refusal of countries throughout the world and the Vatican to "get involved" during the early years of Nazi Germany's reign of terror. We should take the role of people shouting for Jesus to be crucified as we read the Passion because we are still in that position, allowing injustices to occur today. We sometimes act contrary to God's will and do what we know is wrong. We are imperfect, we sin, and we fail to confront evil when we see it.

We need to put a little more pressure on ourselves to be vigilant to prevent evil from taking place and have the strength to act. We need to remember man's inhumanity to man and ask ourselves what we are doing to make sure that those atrocities are never repeated. We must think of ourselves as being there when Christ was crucified and ask ourselves if we would stay with Jesus or run away and hide. C. S. Lewis wrote: "There is no neutral ground in the universe. Every square inch, every split second is claimed by God and counterclaimed by Satan. We must choose."[40]

Effects of a Personal Relationship with God

Our relationship with God changes everything. It defines us. There are no dull, boring or normal situations for us to complain about if every moment becomes a place to put God. With God's assistance, we can create the Kingdom here in how we pack a lunch, walk to the school line with our children, pick them up from school, sit at a desk at work, or go through the checkout line at any store. Every moment becomes an opportunity for doing what Jesus would do and bringing God into this world, even in talking to a neighbor when we pick up our mail.

By turning off the TV and radio, putting down the reading material and focusing our attention on both God and ourselves in each moment what matters to us changes. What is truly important: God's love, becomes clear. Once we acknowledge that we can be next to God, we can look at ourselves, our families, friends, even strangers differently. Maybe when we find the treasure of God's kingdom right around us the trophy case that used to mean so much to us isn't how we measure our value and worth anymore.

Through a personal relationship with God individual relationships change because we're aware of God's presence within everyone. We become discerning and less judgmental seeing possibilities in everyone. We become more active, attempting to create God's kingdom on earth instead of passively awaiting God's kingdom later in heaven. The disorganization of life and the seeming disarray can be seen as the creative process. We become more creative, remembering how creativity results in disorder and that God sees the direction for our lives. The things we thought we needed, such as a car, house, or money, do not hold the same measure of success through God's eyes. Instead, success comes through the satisfaction we feel.

God allows us to see others not as the enemy but as members of the same team. There is no if, no either-or in finding God. Whatever works to bring God into our lives is correct. Feeling the acceptance of God makes us feel open, honest, and if we know peace and contentment, we can be happy regardless of our circumstances in life. Our lives take on a higher value and special meaning as we become motivated and inspired by our relationship with God and realize God is in control.

Who is in control

Trying to figure out what's going on and how God does things, we may feel like a new student in class with God as the teacher. As our picture of God develops, it may become clearer that God is both a teacher *and* a plumber.

Recently I was cleaning out my refrigerator and overestimated the ability of my disposal to deal with large chunks of leftover meat. I assumed that I could simply plop the meat into the disposal and it would be easily shredded and just go away. It never occurred to me that shredded meat would form the perfect filler for pipes much like sawdust can be formed to provide the bulk of flooring or furniture under a thin veneer of wood.

As I was feeding slabs of meat into the sink trying to help the process along, I noticed that when I turned on the disposal, water swirled and splashed everywhere around the sink but did not go down the drain. Even after several minutes I was convinced that the drain would ultimately clear and I could move on to my next project around the house.

Eventually I got a plunger and proceeded to push and pull for a long time, hoping that my next plunge would unclog the drain. Every once in a while the suction action would splatter the dirty water everywhere, but the clog stayed put. By now my wife was aware of the situation and as I was contemplating my next step, she told the kids to stay away from Dad (which I assured her was unnecessary). She also made some flip comment about how she was getting out of there before the cursing started.

Laughingly I assured her it would not come to that. A half an hour later blisters had formed on my hands from the rhythmic tidal-wave motion of the plunging. With backed-up bilge water covering the counters, myself, and the floor, I decided things had reached the next stage and the profanities began to fly freely and loudly.

I wiped up the water and decided to take off the U-bend section of pipe to clean it out but to do so I first had to bail the water out of the sink. I also put a large bucket under the pipe, so when the pipe was loosened enough, the water trapped inside could drain out. Then I cleaned the pipe out, reassembled the section of pipe and repeated the process for what seemed like ten times. When this failed to help, I looked for a snake to clear the pipe. Not finding one, I went to the store and bought one, as well as two huge containers of drain cleaner.

Each time I used the snake, I reattached the pipe and filled the sink back up with water, waiting for some movement in the water level. When none came I began negotiating ways to get out of the situation working out a deal with God. "C'mon, help me out here," I pleaded. Growing weary of this long project, I started questioning God's motivation and began to wonder what God was trying to prove by putting me through this ordeal. Finally, fed up with God and the pipes, I abandoned the project.

Since there were five people in the house, after half of a day the dishes began piling up alarmingly high and I was forced to run the dishwasher. I knew that during the rinse cycles there would be nowhere for the water to go and the kitchen would flood a couple of times if the water wasn't drained. So as the dishwasher ran, I dutifully sat by the sink and bailed out the water into a bucket as it came out, cursing, wondering to myself just who Jesus thought he was.

Because it was clear that God was not going to work with me on this crisis, I plunged (pun intended) into full-fledged melancholy. My depression hit me hard. To pay a plumber a lot of money to come out and unclog our drain was the last thing I needed. The hopelessness of the situation and my inability to deal with it caused me to give up hope, especially since I was painfully aware of my fragile financial situation.

Saturday morning I bit the bullet and called a plumber, only to find that he was not working over the weekend, so I left a message. Even so, I still felt obligated to do more than just observe the problem, knowing full well my efforts were futile. Over the course of the weekend I would peer into the murky brown water in the sink and plunge for a minute or two, even though I knew it wouldn't help; the plumber would come on Monday and this would all be over. Sunday evening I even poured the two bottles of drain-cleaner into the drain, as if making a sacrificial offering to the pipes. It was my final concession to the drain that it had won.

Throughout the weekend, I kept asking God what went wrong. My prayers were not empty words, but emotional, impassioned pleas. Sunday night I tried a few more plunges, and Monday morning I went back to the sink again like a moth drawn to a flame, but nothing happened. Then, after a few more enthusiastic plunges, I stared into the water and swore that I saw a few bubbles coming up from the drain. I was out of hope, but I had to keep doing something. I waited a few minutes, plunged again and thought I saw a few more bubbles. I plunged like crazy and waited a few more seconds to see if the water level was getting lower.

It was.

I tried plunging again with renewed vigor as if I had revived a dying man. As I plunged with enthusiasm, the bubbles kept coming. Then it happened, that beautiful (to me) sucking sound a drain makes when all the water goes out of it. I shrieked with joy as if I had just won something. The rings of backed-up shredded meat left around the edges of the sink reminded me of my own stupidity, but I didn't care; I had my sink back.

As I vowed to never again put meat into the disposal, I tried to figure out what had happened to me over the course of those few days. I was a God-fearing man; why would I have to undergo such trauma? Finally it became clear to me that I had just undergone all the stages of grief. I could also call them my stages of God, or my stages of life.

The first stage is denial and isolation. We can isolate ourselves willingly, deny God's existence and have nothing to do with God, religion, or spirituality while pridefully claiming to be able to run our lives by ourselves, but God remains. We can deny the existence of our problems, set ourselves apart and alone as if we don't need any help pretending we can do it all by ourselves, but God waits with us and the problems remain.

When all the frustration and hostility at not having control of our lives comes out, we look for someone to blame and anger is the next step. There's a lot of energy expended during this stage as we try to fight, cuss, scream and force our way through the crisis. The more we fail, the harder we fight and the more violent we become. As we tell God how to be, we wonder where justice is while being forced to face the fact that we can't control everything that happens to us in our lives. God hadn't clogged my drain; I had.

Bargaining is the next stage where we try to make a deal to work things out. Since we can't take care of problems ourselves, we begrudgingly agree to some help, but with conditions. This is the contract negotiation stage and is followed by depression, which comes from the admission we just can't take care of the problem and that life is not exactly as we would like it to be.

Finally, there is acceptance. Acceptance is the stage where we let God *be* in our lives, when we accept the uncertainty of life and admit we don't control life. Acceptance is the step where we acknowledge that we are driving, but that only God can see the road map of our life. When we allow life to unfold through every interruption rather than trying to force life to be as we desire it to be, we are receptive to God. Peace enters our lives as we allow God to *be* and accept how God works. In the book Healing Words:

> *"Doctor Janet Quinn discovered working with AIDS patients that among the ways they respond one way is to feel completely hopeless and give up. The other was to surrender. Surrendering is incredibly empowering because it is an action. On the other hand,*

giving up is the refusal to take action. To surrender is absolutely active and requires doing over and over again, not once and for all, it's required minute by minute." [41]

Mike had a son about one year old. One evening, when the boy was upstairs in his crib and Mike was watching TV, he heard a terrible gurgling and thrashing sound from up in the baby's room. He ran upstairs and saw the infant convulsing, almost biting his tongue. His eyes were rolled back in his head. The father picked the baby up and screamed for his wife to get the car without even stopping to put his shoes on. Holding the child on the way to the hospital, he put his fingers across the child's teeth to keep him from biting his tongue. Watching the baby shake and shake, Mike started screaming at the baby.

After the hospital took care of the child, the doctors explained he had gone through a "febral seizure." He had a fever and the parents hadn't given him enough Tylenol to bring the fever down, so his body reacted violently. On the way home, Mike's wife told him she couldn't believe the way he was yelling at their little baby when they were on their way to the hospital. Mike told her he wasn't yelling at the baby, he was yelling at God because he thought God was taking his son away. Like Mike, we need to remember we do not control life. We need to accept our role and be thankful for the gift of life that God provides us every day. Maybe then we can see our lives as a tremendous gift, and see that what matters, what is important, is how we live our lives.

CHAPTER TWENTY FIVE

What Matters

Matters of life and death are important, but that's not all that worries us. How upset do we get over spilled coffee, lost keys, or broken fingernails? Sometimes we lose perspective of what is worthy of our concern and what isn't. Our strong emotions over sports contests, reality TV and talk shows might be better channeled into matters of life and death, peace and justice. Maybe the depression and anger we feel when our favorite basketball team loses a big game is a misplaced priority.

We can be touched by movies, shows, or books showing us love, injustice, pain, or wrong-doing. If we become so affected that we cry, why don't we do a better job of seeing emotional, touching situations in our own lives. Why can't we recognize the need to help the people around us?

Watching a movie such as "Love Story" may make us feel so sad that we cry. When the people in any movie are dying, we allow ourselves to feel what they feel and put ourselves in their place. The people in the movie want to touch someone one more time, see someone, hold someone, walk in the rain, or laugh. They want to do the littlest things, the things we forget to appreciate, the things we take for granted.

They are simply more aware of the joy, importance, and meaning of those simple moments. Walking, laughing, holding hands, and enjoying the camaraderie and company of others are the same events that we experience, and it makes us temporarily appreciate how the same ordinary moments of our life can be made extraordinary.

The movie or book is able to present select vivid images and to compress time, comparing and contrasting images and events in ways that real life does not. This technique makes images seem more intense. Our awareness of each moment can make each moment of our lives more intense and challenge what we consider a boring or important occasion. Recognizing that not just the birth of a child, graduation day, or award ceremony are important events, but the seemingly random instances like holding grandpa's hand or the fight we had with our sister when we were twelve, those are opportunities for us to remember them and appreciate because of the awareness we gave to the moment.

The composer Giacomo Puccini died of throat cancer while writing his last opera, <u>Turandot</u>, leaving it unfinished. Puccini begged his friends to finish the piece if he died before completing the work, and his friend Arturo Toscanini conducted the first performance of the opera. While performing the piece, when Toscanini reached the point where the composer died, he stopped, turned to the audience and said, "This is where the master ends." After a moment of reflection and silence, he said, "And this is where his friends began." Then he continued with the rest of the piece. Similarly, we must continue on after a loss. We believe we will see our friends and family in heaven so the best thing we can do to remember them is to carry on with our lives, continuing the work they have begun.

We can't avoid death and change, and we can't hide from death or change. Worrying about the inevitable won't do us any good. Death is a part of our lives, death is a fact. If we fear death, it's only natural to want to avoid talking about it. A well-known sportswriter, Red Smith, once said at a friend's funeral, "Dying is no big deal. The least among us will manage that; it's living that's the trick."

Many people who have a brush with death are affected so much that afterward they attempt to live every single moment as fully as possible with a renewed sense of purpose, realizing how precious and fleeting life is. If we were told that this was our last day on earth or that we had only a few months to live, we might wake up seeing every day as a gift and pay more attention to how we live it. The best preparation for our death is living a life we find meaningful.

For people who do not believe in heaven, death means it's all over and their existence is finished. That finality is sad. For those of us who believe in God, death marks the end of this stage of our existence and the beginning of the afterlife. If we believe in God, death is no tragedy because we end up at our final destination. Death cannot take our future away; only we can lose that gift by turning our back on God. Like Father Bart Smith said during mass, for we who believe in God, the worst possibility is not death; the worst possible thing that could happen would be for us to lose our salvation.

Free will and God's grace are always available to us and always here with us. If we see ourselves as second grade children walking to school, God walks us all the way to the school building and doesn't just drop us off. If we see a friend or classmate and want to go run off and see them, God lets us. If we want to hold hands, God holds our hand. God, like an aware parent, allows us to be independent while still being available to us as our anchor. If God takes us to the park or beach, God doesn't tell us when we have to leave, either. God lets us wait until we say we want to go home. God doesn't ever abandon us either, even after death.

Application

Richard Cardinal Cushing said, "For centuries now we've tried everything else; the power of wealth, of mighty armies and navies, machinations of diplomats. All have failed. Before it's too late, and time is running out, let us turn from trust in the chain reactions of exploding atoms to faith in the chain reaction of God's love. Love-love of God and fellow men. That is God's formula for peace. Peace on earth to men of good will." In John 14:23-29, Jesus said to his disciples:

> *"Whoever loves me will keep my word, and my Father will love him, and we will come to him and make our dwelling with him. Whoever does not love me does not keep my words; yet the word you hear is not mine but that of the Father who sent me.*
>
> *"I have told you this while I am with you. The Advocate, the Holy Spirit, whom the Father will send in your name, will teach you everything and remind you of all that I told you. Peace I leave with you; my peace I give to you. Not as the world gives do I give it to you. Do not let your hearts be troubled or afraid. You heard me tell you, 'I am going away and I will come back to you.' If you loved me, you would rejoice that I am going to the Father; for the Father is greater than I. And now I have told you this before it happens, so that when it happens you may believe."*

After three years of following Jesus, his disciples didn't want to hear how everything was going to be changing for them. After being a part of Jesus' ministry, they would no longer be with him and their lives would no longer be the same. The apostles were losing their comfort zone, but being uncomfortable can be good because it can give rise to action.

Jesus was telling his disciples that he had to go away. If Jesus stayed with the disciples the only people who could be with Jesus were the people who were in the same physical place Jesus was. By changing form to the Holy Spirit, Jesus allows all believers to experience God at every church on every Sunday and in every interaction every day. At Pentecost the apostles were in a room huddled together, scared and unsure. The Holy Spirit came upon them and they became bold, strong, and unafraid. They became aware and sure of what they were doing. We have the same Holy Spirit available to us to make us bold, strong, and unafraid of change and enable us to do God's will.

Sometimes we resist change because we become too comfortable, but change is not something to be afraid of but embraced. God is not confined to one place and time but is continuously experienced and part of history, not only two thousand years ago but every day and every moment. God is part of our history today, here and now, sending us out to spread the message of salvation and love while assuring us that the Holy Spirit will always be with us to give us strength and direction to guide us.

God can make us feel better than sex or any drug can make us feel, and the feeling God gives us does not go away. We have the opportunity to fill our lives with instances of love, instants of love. Those are our trophies; they are the substance of what we accomplish. The image, the physical trophy, is only the idea, but the creation of God's kingdom is what is important. God gives us the chance to make as many instants of love as we can and sends us out with only our faith to assure us that we will be provided with everything we need if we are rooted in Heaven.

On a retreat (a time of reflection and examination of life) during his junior year in high school, a boy named Matt walked into the retreat center chapel for the closing liturgy and found it filled with people from previous retreats who had come to share the experience with the retreatants.

Matt listened attentively as the retreat director, Father Paul, spoke to the retreatants at the conclusion of the liturgy. All of the individuals were feeling so good and so alive that many of them didn't want the retreat to end. Father told the students not to be reluctant to leave and go back to the "real world." He told them that the retreat *was* the real world. The retreat showed the students the intensity of feelings they could experience and how loving and accepting people could be of one another in an environment of trust, awareness, and concern. He told them the challenge was to take the real world of the retreat back to the other world and try to make both places one and the same.

Because he had grown comfortable with the other individuals on the retreat, Matt initially didn't want those other people there. He felt a little sad knowing that his retreat family was no longer the same; it had changed. Then he realized his challenge was to see both groups as the same family, only larger. God must be put in this world we have. Mahatma Gandhi said, "I am part and parcel of the whole, and I cannot find God apart of the rest of humanity."

Creating Heaven and Seeing God

God's hand is always open toward us, giving us the opportunity to open our hand back in acceptance. Our job is to reply to the invitation and open ourselves to God. There is so much work to be done to create the kingdom and so many people in so much need that God needs us to minister to neighbors we feed, care for, clothe, and help when they need assistance. We might think we're not worthy, but the job must be done. It's not someone else's job, it is ours. What an awesome responsibility and what an amazing opportunity. Just as Jesus did with the loaves and fishes, God will make our every effort more than enough.

Our ultimate achievement is being great, being the best. In Mark 10:35 it says,

"The greatest in the kingdom of Heaven must be the servant of all the others." Our greatest achievement is to serve, not be served and to do our best imitation of God.

A little girl asked her daddy how he knew there was a God. He answered that he knew there was a God and God was real because he had experienced God and felt heaven. He told the little girl when he was in sixth grade, he remembered leaving his basketball practice at Holy Family grade school in Hillcrest Heights, Maryland on a cold, dark winter evening when he noticed Michael, a 20 year old mentally retarded neighbor of his, leaving the gym at the same time.

The girl's father said that he decided to walk home with Michael and make sure Michael made it home safely. Even though he was always a little afraid when he walked home, this evening he felt the opposite of afraid, he felt protected, and as though he was not alone. Years later he realized that because he chose to think about Michael, it seemed as though God and all the angels in heaven went along with them on their walk home. What he experienced then was the kingdom of Heaven and the indescribable contentment and peace he felt was from God. He told his daughter that he constantly attempts to attain that feeling again, to taste, feel, and hear God again by trying to act out of selfless concern for others.

The kingdom is here among us. Can we see it? Every moment we have the opportunity to experience God and Heaven. We can spend our time making heaven and seeing God. We can give our next interaction great attentiveness and love and treat the next person we see as if they were God. Through our attention to the divine nature of every instant, we can find God and give critical importance to every moment. If God isn't in this moment it's because we haven't allowed God to enter it through us. We are builders of the kingdom. We are the ones who must bring God to the world this instant, not only on our wedding day or when our children are born, but in how we prepare for work today.

What if Heaven is a level of love to be reached? What if God's level of absolute love, care, selflessness, and concern for another person is a layer to be broken through like the huge paper banner a football team breaks through before the homecoming game? Then Heaven can be attained through our actions as a result of our love. That level of love is the kingdom Jesus spoke about when he told the apostles that it was among them but they did not see it.

We can create Heaven when certain conditions are met, when we focus complete and unrestricted love on others and turn our consciousness and awareness toward the best interest of another person. Religious individuals can seem a little out of touch with reality, but with one hand on earth and one hand in Heaven, maybe they realize the perfection of God's kingdom is possible through the visible reality of our actions. Heaven isn't something we have to wait until later to experience; we can create and experience Heaven right now, here on earth.

To relieve human suffering in any way is the greatest expression of God's love. Maybe that is why seeing a child laugh is one of the clearest pictures of Heaven we may ever see. Every time any human has lovingly held a dying person or cradled a child, God was present and Heaven was realized in that space.

People who show love seem to be at peace because they're attempting to create or allow Heaven to be expressed in that moment; they're busy making Heaven. Every time we assist another person, we are claiming that instant for God. Maybe that's why so many representations of Heaven depict movement in slow motion: so every second can be claimed by God.

St. Ignatius Loyola was a Spanish nobleman who founded the Jesuit order of Catholic priests and based the order on Seven Principle Elements of Ignatian Spirituality.

One of those elements is that God is in all things, that God is present in all of human existence. Another element is, if God can be found in all things, human beings can discern God's presence in the world. Still another element is that the person in front of me is the most important person in the world.

If we take this last thought a step further, we have the ability to bring God into all of human existence and all things. We may have been told all our lives that, "It is not about you." Well, it *is* about us, 100%. Making God's kingdom here on earth is a job that can only be done by us, and we must create that kingdom through our actions. Our life is not something that happens to us or something we do, it is *every*thing we do.

Many doctors encourage ill people to make a list of things to accomplish before they die, such as climb a mountain, take a cruise, travel to exotic places, or visit every continent in the world. That list can also contain things that we can attain right now, like bringing God to the moment and creating Heaven while at work with co-workers, at school with teachers, with students in class, at home as we clean up the family room or with the people in front of us and behind us in the checkout line at the store.

Our job for God is not specified and we are free to choose what we do. We might be a good listener, have a green thumb, or be a great cook. Maybe we have a rapport with children, or the elderly. We can focus our attention to look directly into the eyes of another person, listen to every word that person says to us and consider how best to serve their needs by bringing God into the love we bring into that moment. Service is not only the 40 hours of community service work we did to fulfill our high school requirement, but the attention we give to the needs of those people we are looking at right now.

The limits of Heaven on earth is how often we can create it and for as long as we can create it. The only way to express the kingdom is to hook together all the pieces of Heaven we can create so they connect and touch, like a beautifully knitted quilt. The job itself is not as important as how we do it. Contrary to the preoccupation of religion with *how* we serve and worship God, God seems to be reciting the quote hanging on the wall of my father-in-law's office: "I have no interest in how it can't be done."

What if Jesus showed up at our door right now? Instead of thinking about what we would say to him and wondering how we would react, we would do better to consider our life as a preparation for just such a meeting. The whole point of seeing God in all those people we come in contact with every day is to increase our familiarity and comfort level with God and treat them with the same care, concern, and consideration as we would treat Jesus himself if we were to recognize him on the street dressed in rags. Jesuit Alphonsus Rodriguez served at Montesion College in Majorca, Spain for 24 years beginning in 1571. In his memoirs, he wrote that every time the door was knocked upon, he would reply, "I'm coming, Lord" reminding himself that every knock was a knock from God.

What if Jesus actually did knock on our door today, spoke to us and said, "I unconditionally love you more than anything else in the world; please help me." As awesome as the possibility of actually seeing God face to face may seem, and even though it can lead us to intense spiritual introspection, shouldn't we react like we would if a friend came to visit us and shouldn't we react to every knock on our door as if it was Jesus?

We could bend over, bow, or kneel in worship to honor God, and God might appreciate our acknowledgment. We could try to impress him with our trophy case or possessions, but what really matters is our *service*. Isn't it time we stand up, look up with joyfully outstretched arms, invite Jesus in and consider how we can help him? Shouldn't we respond to God as we should respond to those around us, by asking, "What can I do for you?"

Bibliography

Page

1. 9 There is Another Way to Live
       Parade Magazine November 30, 2003
       Dodson Rader

2. 20 A World Waiting to Be Born M. Scott
       Peck p 46 Bantam Books 1993

3. 24 The World's Religions Huston Smith
       p 113 Harper San Francisco 1991

4. 27 The Pain of Christ and the Sorrow of
       God Gerald Vannp p 54-55 Temple
       Gate Publishers Springfield, Illinois
       Copyright by Aquin Press 1947
Cited in People of the Lie M. Scott Peck p 73
       Simon & Schuster 1983

5. 27   People of the Lie M. Scott Peck p 67
          Simon & Schuster 1983

          The Great Divorce C.S. Lewis
          New York, Macmillan 1946
    Cited in People of the Lie M. Scott Peck
          Simon & Schuster 1983

6. 37   Affair Statistics by Karen S. Peterson
          USA Today 1998 item from Smart
          Marriages Archive Reproduced by
          Divorce Statistics Collection

7. 37   (http://www.divorcereform.org/mel/
          raffairstats.html)

8. 37   (http://www.aboutlovers.co.za/stats.
          html) William Mitchell Eagles Nest
          Publications 2001 Divorce Facing its
          Reality

9. 61   The Road Less Traveled M. Scott Peck
          p 51 Simon & Schuster 1978

10. 62   World Waiting to be Born M. Scott
          Peck Bantam Books p 76, 91, 112, 128,
          142, 175, 191, 261.

11. 66   The Historical Jesus John Dominic
          Crossan p 4 Harper Collins 1991

12. 67   The Historical JesusJohn Dominic
           Crossan p 115 Harper Collins 1991
           Citing Jewish Historian Josephus
           Jewish Antiquities 18.23-24

13. 70   The World's ReligionsHuston Smith
           p 331 Harper San Francisco 1991

14. 71   Jesus E. Schillebeeckx p 201 Crossroad
           New York 1981
    Cited in   The World's Religions Huston Smith
           p 332 Harper San Francisco 1991

15. 75   The Prophet Kahlil Gibran p 13 Alfred
           A. Knopf 1923

16. 77   The Path to Love Deepak Chopra
           Deepak Chopra 1997

17. 113   I & Thou Martin Buber Charles
           Scribner & Sons New York 1970
           translated Walter Kaufmann

18. 119   The Prophet Kahlil Gibran p 16 Alfred
           A. Knopf 1923

19. 128   Getting Your Manuscript Sold Sterling
           Davidson p 10 Barclay House 1995

20. 131   Collected Letters of St. Therese of
           Lisieux translation F.J. Sheed p 303
           Sheed and Ward, 1949

Cited in   People of the Lie M. Scott Peck p 11
                 Simon & Schuster 1983

21. 141   Healing Words Larry Dossey p122
                 Harper Collins 1993

22. 144   Aldous Huxley's proposed Law of
                 Reversed Effort
Cited in   Healing Words Larry Dossey p 117
                 Harper Collins 1993

23. 145   Healing WordsLarry Dossey p 291
                 Harper Collins 1993

24. 146   Prayer Can Change Your Life William
                 Parker & Elaine St. John's Prentiss Hall
                 Press New York 1957
Cited in   Healing Words Larry Dossey p 238-9
                 Harper Collins 1993

25. 146   Healing Words Larry Dossey p 289
                 Harper Collins 1993

26. 147   Healing Words Larry Dossey p 288
                 Harper Collins 1993

27. 147   Healing Words Larry Dossey p 289
                 Harper Collins 1993

28. 166   People of the Lie M. Scott Peck p 83
                 Simon & Schuster 1983

29. 171 Alcohol Statistics Traffic Safety Facts 2001 National Highway Safety Administration (April 2001) Setting Limits, Saving Lives: The Case for .08 BAC Laws Washington DC US Department of Transportation

30. 186 The World's Religions Huston Smith p328 Harper San Francisco 1991

31. 192 World Waiting to be Born 1993 M. Scott Peck p 358 Bantam Books

32. 196 The World's Religions Huston Smith p 82 Harper San Francisco 1991

33. 248 Christianity and the Constitution John Eidsmoe p 369 Baker Book House 1987

34. 252 World Waiting to be Born M. Scott Peck p 53 Bantam Books 1993

35. 254 World Waiting to be Born M. Scott Peck p 127-128 Bantam Books 1993

36. 265 People of the Lie M. Scott Peck p 204 Simon & Schuster 1983

37. 273 Spoken at Georgetown Preparatory School Father Son Dinner April 2003

38. 283 Mensa Magazine Gary Eisler 2001

39. 292   World Waiting to be Born M. Scott
Peck p 48 Bantam Books 1993

40. 298   Christianity and Culture contained in
Christian Reflections, edited by William
Hooper Wm B. Eerdmans Publishing
co., Grand Rapids 1967 p 33

  Cited in   People of the Lie M. Scott Peck p 83
C. S. Lewis quote

41. 305   Dennis Gersten M.D. Interview with
Janet Quinn, R.n. Ph.D., "AIDS, Hope
and Healing," Part II Atlantis, The
Imagery Newsletter Feb 1992 3 ff.
  Cited in   Healing Words Larry Dossey p138
Harper Collins 1993

Printed in the United States
55136LVS00001B/1-54

9 781597 819794